# HOW ECONOMICS WORKS

# HOW ECONOMICS WORKS

## The CONCEPTS visually explained

**Project Editor** Daniel Byrne
**Project Art Editor** Daksheeta Pattni
**Editors** John Andrews, Claire Cross, Elizabeth Dowsett,
Victoria Heyworth-Dunne, Alison Sturgeon,
Andrew Szudek, Alex Whittleton
**Senior US Editor** Kayla Dugger
**Executive US Editor** Lori Cates Hand
**Illustrators** Mark Clifton,
Vanessa Hamilton, Mark Lloyd
**Managing Editor** Gareth Jones
**Managing Art Editor** Lee Griffiths
**Production Editor** Robert Dunn
**Production Controller** Nancy-Jane Maun
**Jacket Designer** Tanya Mehrotra
**Senior DTP Designer** Harish Aggarwal
**Senior Jackets Coordinator** Priyanka Sharma Saddi
**Jacket Design Development Manager** Sophia MTT
**Publisher** Liz Wheeler
**Publishing Director** Jonathan Metcalf
**Art Director** Karen Self

First American Edition, 2024
Published in the United States by DK Publishing,
a division of Penguin Random House LLC
1745 Broadway, 20th Floor, New York, NY 10019

A catalog record for this book
is available from the Library of Congress.
ISBN 978-0-7440-9853-2

Printed in the UAE

www.dk.com

This book was made with Forest
Stewardship Council™ certified
paper – one small step in DK's
commitment to a sustainable future.
Learn more at **www.dk.com/uk/
information/sustainability**

CONTENTS

# MACROECONOMICS

# SCHOOLS OF ECONOMIC THOUGHT

## CONSULTANT

**Peter Antonioni** is a lecturer in the Department of Management Science and Innovation at UCL, where he teaches the economics of media and information sectors. He holds a BA in philosophy, politics, and economics from the University of Oxford and an MSc in economics from Birkbeck College, London. Peter is co-author of *Economics for Dummies* and was the consultant for DK's *Simply Economics*.

## CONTRIBUTORS

**Michael Ashby** is a college associate professor of economics at Downing College, University of Cambridge. He teaches econometrics, finance, quantitative methods, and macroeconomics. Michael is Downing's Director of Studies in Economics and is a Fellow of the College. He holds BA, MPhil, and PhD degrees in economics from the University of Cambridge.

# INTERNATIONAL TRADE

# FINANCE

**John Farndon** is a London-based author, poet, and translator. He has written more than 1,000 books and been shortlisted for Young People's Science Book Prize five times. He has contributed to DK's *The Economics Book: Big Ideas Simply Explained, Economics For Kids,* and *Simply Economics.*

**Andrew Szudek** is a writer and editor who studied philosophy at the University of Cambridge, where he focused on political philosophy and ethics. He has worked on numerous nonfiction titles, ranging from economics to military history.

**Marcus Weeks** has written and contributed to numerous books on politics, philosophy, psychology, and the arts, including *Heads Up Money* and several titles in DK's *Big Ideas* series. He was also a contributor for DK's *How Politics Works* and the consultant for *How Philosophy Works.*

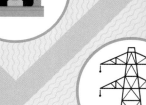

# INTRODUCTION

Economic news is at least as prominent as political news. Governments and national leaders can be replaced, sometimes with astonishing swiftness. This is not because they upset political allies or fail to defend their countries' borders. Instead, it is often due to their mishandling handling of public finances: underestimating inflation, causing a run on their currency, or crashing the stock market. Such events or processes are difficult to fathom without at least some knowledge of economics. When world-changing events, such as the global financial crisis of 2007–2008, turn out to be rooted in transactions involving "credit default swaps," "collateralized debt obligations," or other mysterious financial "instruments," even professional investors are puzzled.

However, economics is not just about governments and financial experts, but also households and businesses. These groups are all driven by the same basic financial forces—the need to have the resources (money, in particular) to buy and sell products and services, and to control those resources. The origin of the word "economics" is itself uncomplicated—it comes from the ancient Greek term *oikonomia*, or "household management." So behind what can often seem like impenetrable technical jargon, economists essentially study how to live within a budget while maximizing prosperity—something that is as important for individuals and their families as it is for nation-states and major corporations.

*How Economics Works* provides an accessible overview of economic theory and demystifies the key concepts of finance. Chapter 1 defines the basic terms used in economics, such as "scarcity," "utility," and "rational choice," while chapters 2 and 3 explain how markets work (microeconomics) and how governments run their economies (macroeconomics). Chapters 4 to 6 look at different schools of economic thought and at international trade and finance.

# FUNDAMENTALS OF ECONOMICS

Economics is rooted in fundamental concepts such as scarcity, utility, and rationality. Economists use these as tools to analyze how individuals and societies make choices when resources are limited.

# What is economics?

**Economics is the study of how goods and services are produced and delivered and why individuals, businesses, and governments make the spending decisions they do.**

## Scarcity

Central to economics is the notion of "scarcity," or "being in short supply" (see pp.14–15). If everyone always had what they wanted, there could be no economists, because economists study demand (what people want) and supply (what people produce), both of which are reactions to scarcity. Because people have wants or needs, there is a market (see pp. 34–35) for what they lack—which means an opportunity for producers to supply it. Likewise, producers require things such as premises and equipment to produce their goods, which are opportunities for more producers. The "economy" is the total number of exchanges between consumers and producers in a given area—which could be local or global—and includes a whole host of contracts between

## Microeconomics and macroeconomics

Economics is divided into two main subjects: microeconomics and macroeconomics. Microeconomics is concerned with individual consumers and businesses and the financial decisions they make. Macroeconomics focuses on the behavior and performance of the economy as a whole, including how governments try to steer the economy by raising or lowering taxes and controlling the money supply.

PURCHASES AND LABOR

WAGES

### MICROECONOMICS

Looking at society from the bottom up, microeconomics analyzes how individual people, firms, and households make decisions and respond to changes in the price and availability of goods.

**Individuals and households**
Individual people and households earn money by selling their labor to producers, who pay them wages.

**Firms**
Businesses depend on the labor of the individuals who produce the goods they sell. They sell to make a profit, or at least to break even.

investors (who lend money) and firms and all of the economic activity stimulated by taxation and government spending policies.

## Developing resources

Today, economists advise firms and governments on how to raise, invest, and spend money most efficiently, but also, more broadly, on how to allocate financial resources, such as profits and tax revenues, to maximize prosperity. They also tend to specialize in particular fields, such as industrial or labor economics.

## INDUSTRIAL ECONOMICS

This is the study of firms, industries, and markets of all sizes, from corner stores to giant multinationals. Key areas include how and why firms advertise, how much firms invest in research and development, and the levels at which prices are set.

## LABOR ECONOMICS

This is the study of the labor force as an element of the production process. Key areas include how pension reforms, education, childcare, and pay affect the lives of workers.

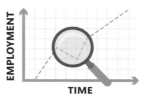

**NATIONAL ECONOMY**

### Government
The government's fiscal (taxation) and monetary (money supply) policies shape the overall economy.

+

### Aggregate markets
The aggregate economy is everything that people produce and consume. The total supply and total demand levels of markets change depending on whether the economy is growing or shrinking.

> "Economics is, at root, the study of incentives: how people get what they want, or need."
>
> Steven D. Levitt, American economist, and Stephen J. Dubner, American journalist, *Freakonomics* (2005)

### International trade
Modern economies depend on international trade. Nations generally aim to export (sell) more than they import (buy).

## MACROECONOMICS

Looking at society from the top down, macroeconomics studies how economies perform as a whole, analyzing "aggregate" (total) changes to key economic features such as prices and employment levels.

# Scarcity

**If something is scarce, there is not enough of it to fulfill everyone's needs and wants. Without scarcity, people would have all they desired and there would be no trading—and no economy.**

## Scarcity requires trade-offs

Some resources, such as air, are effectively infinite, but most are not. For example, money, time, and raw materials are all limited, but our demand for them is theoretically unlimited. Whenever scarcity arises, decision-making and trade-offs become inevitable, and using a scarce resource prevents it from being used for another purpose or by someone else. Scarcity has various causes (see opposite) and plays a significant role in producers' decisions about what to produce (see below) to ensure sufficient demand. All decisions about scarce resources made by individuals, firms, and other organizations interact to create the economy.

## The role of the market

When the market—the trade of goods and services—is shaped by supply and demand (see pp.44–45), one way to decide who gets which scarce resources is price. If a scarce item is in high demand, sellers can raise its price, but only as far as potential buyers will pay.

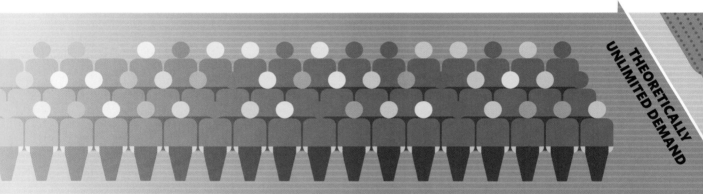

THEORETICALLY UNLIMITED DEMAND

## The allocation of resources

Scarcity forces people to make choices about how to allocate resources. Firms decide what to produce, and consumers decide what to buy. In a command economy, the state decides (see p.32), but even in economies shaped by supply and demand (see pp.44–45), these decisions can be political, and sometimes governments play a role (see pp.108–109).

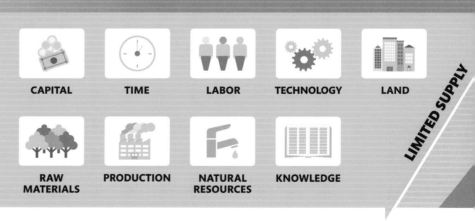

| CAPITAL | TIME | LABOR | TECHNOLOGY | LAND |
| RAW MATERIALS | PRODUCTION | NATURAL RESOURCES | KNOWLEDGE | |

LIMITED SUPPLY

**Imbalance**
The gap between people's theoretically unlimited wants (demand) and the limited resources (supply) available to meet them leads to scarcity.

# "Economics is the science which studies human behavior as a relationship between ends and scarce means."

Lionel Robbins, British economist,
*The Nature and Significance of Economic Science* (1935)

### What to produce
Scarcity plays a key part in determining what producers choose to supply—they will not produce sand for the Sahara. Instead, they select a product that is scarce and in demand.

### Scarcity
There is not enough of something for everyone to be satisfied, so decisions must be made about who gets what.

### How to produce
Producers must work out the best way to use their resources. For example, the extreme rarity and value of some metals used in batteries might make it worth investing in sourcing them.

### Who to produce for
Producers need to identify where there is a scarcity. The Netherlands can supply Europe with flowers in summer, but there is scarcity in winter, which Zimbabwean growers can meet.

## CAUSES OF SCARCITY

### Demand-induced scarcity
Here, the demand for a resource increases while the supply stays the same. Demand could be fueled by population growth or by a product, such as the latest toy that everyone wants at Christmas.

### Supply-induced scarcity
In this case, demand stays the same but supply dwindles. Supply could be reduced because of crop failure or deforestation. "Limited edition" items are an example of producers intentionally reducing supply.

### Structural scarcity
This occurs where some people have less access to resources than others. It can be political or due to location—for example, people in a village may have less access to healthcare than those in a city.

# Utility

Economists use "utility" to describe the benefit or satisfaction that a product or service provides to a consumer. How much utility a person expects to receive influences their economic decisions.

## Measuring utility

The utility of consuming, for example, a particular food could be physical benefits like satisfying hunger or providing nutrition. It also includes feelings, such as altruism for supporting an independent café or superiority for being seen at a fashionable restaurant. Utility can also be reduced by negative feelings, such as guilt for eating unhealthily.

Although utility is an abstract concept, and hard to measure in terms of exactly how much benefit a person receives, the idea has endured in economics. Originally, economists believed in "cardinal utility"—the thought that utility can be measured in units called "utils," allowing for the mathematical analysis of economic behaviours. However, consumers may not be able to evaluate their received utility accurately. The measure of utility also varies from person to person and even for the same person. Sometimes, utility reduces as more units of an item are consumed (see pp.20–21).

## Relative utility

Few economists now believe utility can be quantified. Instead, they may talk about "ordinal utility," which ranks utility. For example, if a consumer prefers

## Comparing utility

Even when two people buy an identical product or service, it is unlikely that they will experience the same level of utility. Their varying needs mean they gain different levels of usefulness, and their diverse preferences and tastes will determine how much they enjoy their purchase.

### Low utility

Shopper A lives in a mostly warm and dry climate, so she will only use the coat occasionally. She is not very concerned about what it looks like or how well it suits her.

SHOPPER A

One util of satisfaction

### The utility of a coat

As well as the practical need for a coat and any aesthetic preferences, other factors may affect the utility a consumer gets from a coat.

> **Fit** The desire to be comfortable and the level of concern for how well the coat fits and complements the individual's appearance.
> **Material** The preference for a particular type of fabric—for example, the desire to wear high-tech fabrics or natural fibers.
> **Social responsibility** The desire to shop ethically and limit environmental impact.
> **Price** The satisfaction of getting a bargain or the enjoyment of making an extravagant purchase.

watching ballet to football, ballet has greater utility than football, but it is not possible to say by how much. All the same, utility may reveal the changing levels of satisfaction behind consumer choices and subsequently their spending patterns, which is useful for economists and also for firms wanting to better understand their customers.

> "Nothing can have **value** without being an **object** of utility."

Karl Marx, German economist, *Das Kapital, Volume 1* (1867)

## PRICE VS. VALUE

Price is the amount of money a buyer pays for an item. Value, like utility, is how useful the item is to the buyer or how much it means to them, which can be influenced by factors such as quality, brand, and customer experience. The American investor Warren Buffet (b. 1930) famously said, "Price is what you pay; value is what you get."

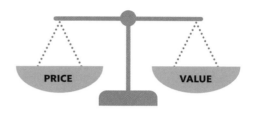

PRICE    VALUE

## High utility

Shopper B lives in a cold and rainy climate, so he has great need for a warm and waterproof coat. He also takes great pride in his appearance, so will get a lot of satisfaction from feeling good about how he looks.

SHOPPER B

Three utils of satisfaction

## Types of utilities

Behavioral economics (see pp.146–147) recognizes that there may be different measures of utility for the same product.

**FORM UTILITY**

How well a product satisfies a customer's needs; for example, it could be the price or the design of a product.

**TIME UTILITY**

How well the availability of a product matches when it is needed. For example, does overnight delivery matter?

**PLACE UTILITY**

How easily customers can access goods or services in a suitable location—for example, a good website.

**POSSESSION UTILITY**

How useful a product is for a consumer to own—for example, summer shorts are little use in snowy weather.

# Rational choice

In economics, the concept of rationality is closely related to that of self-interest: an individual's choice is rational, whether as a consumer or in business, when it brings them the most benefit.

## Self-interest

The majority of early economic theory was based on the idea that economies can be explained as the combined effect of people making logical decisions in their own self-interest. A shopper may choose to buy goods from one store instead of another based on price. On the other hand, someone looking for a job might choose one that maximizes leisure time over pay. In his 1776 book *The Wealth of Nations*, Adam Smith (1723–1790) argued that, taken together, the rational, self-interested decisions made by all individuals act like an invisible hand that steers the economy toward the best possible outcome (see pp.126–127). This idea developed into "rational choice theory."

Many 20th-century economists used rational choice theory not only to explain how economies worked, but to create "models" that predicted outcomes. In these models, economic decisions are made by "individual utility maximizers" (individuals who seek the most benefit for themselves), or what some economists named *Homo economicus* ("economic man")—an ideal individual who makes economic choices rationally.

## Always acting rationally?

In recent years, rational choice theory has been criticized on many grounds. Some theorists challenge it for ethical reasons, claiming that self-interest is not the prime motivator of human behavior. Others claim that it fails to reflect reality, because people do not always act "rationally." Behavioral economics (see pp.146–147) is a field that was developed partly to correct these limitations.

**Assumption 1**
Individuals know what they want, which might be more money or more quality.

## Making assumptions

In economic terms, rationality is a theoretical model that is based on a set of assumptions about how individuals make rational choices that bring them the most benefit. These assumptions are not descriptions of reality, but premises that enable economies to be analyzed mathematically. This mathematical framework underpins the growing use of computer predictions of economic outcomes that many governments rely on today.

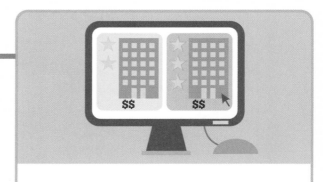

**Assumption 4**
Individuals seek the maximum utility (the most good, or benefit) for themselves.

"When faced with several courses of action, people usually do what they believe is likely to have the best overall outcome."

Jon Elster, Norwegian philosopher, *Social Norms and Economic Theory* (1989)

**Assumption 2**
Individuals tend to rank their preferences, deciding, for instance, to choose low-cost over luxury.

**Assumption 3**
Based on their preferences, individuals can make a logical choice between various options.

**Assumption 5**
Individuals have consistent preferences, so their behavior is predictable.

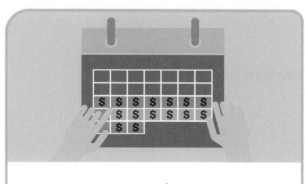

**Assumption 6**
Individuals try to avoid anything that gets in the way of their preferred choice.

# Marginalism

**Marginalism is the economic principle that people make economic decisions bit by bit instead of all in one go. In economics, what matters is the next, incremental decision.**

## Market observations

The concept of marginalism was developed in the late 19th century by three European economists: Carl Menger (1840–1921), William Stanley Jevons (1835–1882), and Léon Walras (1834–1910). While looking at how goods were valued in the market, they noticed that prices were inconsistent; a pound of apples did not always cost the same. They realized that what matters is how much more people want something at a particular moment. This crucial insight finally explained the "diamond–water paradox" (see right) that had been puzzling economists for a century.

The price of something depends not on its overall value, but on its "marginal utility"—how much benefit (or "utility," see pp.16–17) one more unit will provide.

## Diminishing marginal utility

Marginal utility depends on the priorities of the buyer at that moment. A cup of coffee might be vital to start the day, but a second cup may be less appealing, and a third might be too much—even though each coffee is the same. People will pay the most for the first cup but less for each subsequent cup. This is the idea of "diminishing marginal utility." Sometimes, there is

## Unit by unit

Buyers weigh the marginal utility of consuming additional goods against their marginal cost—the extra cost incurred for each additional unit. While marginal utility diminishes with each unit, marginal costs gradually rise. According to the theory, consumers stop additional purchases when the marginal costs exceed the marginal utility.

1ST    2ND

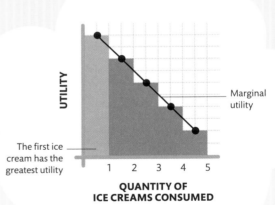

UTILITY

Marginal utility

The first ice cream has the greatest utility

1  2  3  4  5

**QUANTITY OF ICE CREAMS CONSUMED**

### Marginal utility

In the case of consuming ice creams, the first ice cream may bring great pleasure, but the enjoyment diminishes with each one—this might be because the consumer gradually tires of the taste or feels full.

# "Every successive unit gives utility with a diminishing rate."

Alfred Marshall, British economist, *Principles of Economics* (1890)

a threshold before it applies. When collecting signed sports jerseys, the utility of each might increase until the full set is collected, then it will drop to zero.

The realization that price depends on marginal utility led to the theories of supply and demand (see pp.44–45). Walras was inspired to create the first supply curve (see p.43) and demand curve (see p.41). Price is determined by where these two curves intersect. At this point, the market is said to be "in equilibrium."

## CASE STUDY

### The diamond–water paradox

In his 1776 work *The Wealth of Nations*, the Scottish economist Adam Smith (1723–1790) presented an apparent paradox in how the market reflects value. Because water is vital to survival, why does it cost much less, unit for unit, than diamonds, which are beautiful but relatively useless? A century later, the theory of marginal utility neatly resolved this paradox. Overall, the value of water is immense compared to diamonds. The first few units may even save your life, and beyond drinking it, we need large quantities for growing food, cooking, and washing. However, as water is plentiful and diamonds are scarce, the marginal value of a unit of diamonds far exceeds the marginal value of a unit of water.

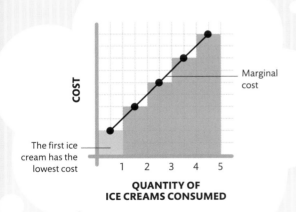

### Marginal cost

Ice creams have a financial cost, and too many might make a consumer sick or bring health issues, so their marginal cost increases with each one.

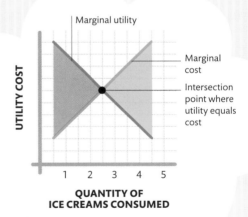

### Utility versus cost

The marginal utility for consumers decreases with each extra ice cream, while the marginal costs rise. When marginal costs equals marginal utility, the consumer stops receiving satisfaction from consuming an additional ice cream.

# Opportunity cost

**Whenever consumers make a purchase choice, they reject other options that might have given them greater benefits. Economists call the cost of these lost opportunities "opportunity cost."**

## Weighing the alternatives

Whenever individuals choose to buy a product or service, they lose out on the potential advantages of an alternative choice. For example, someone might want to travel somewhere either by car or train. The car is the cheaper and more convenient option, but there are opportunity costs in missing out on the time to read and relax that the train offers.

The concept of opportunity cost acknowledges that besides the short-term monetary cost of a choice, there are less explicit longer-term costs in the choice that is not made—such as time, effort, and wear and tear. By accounting for these costs, individuals and firms can maximize the benefits of their economic decisions. For example, suppose a firm is making an investment in capital that will bring in a profit of $1 million, but an alternative option is leaving the money in a bank to accrue $2 million in interest. In this case, the profit from the capital is a loss of $1 million after opportunity cost.

## Counting the cost

The costs involved in a choice are not always easy to evaluate, nor are they always a question of money. If a firm offers its workers three hours of overtime a week, those employees will get three hours' extra pay by accepting the offer, but they will also incur a cost in leisure time lost. On the other hand, if the workers turn down the offer, they might miss out on the chance to build up savings and investments (see pp.186–187) that earn them more leisure time in the long term.

## Is it worth it?

A driver has a choice of two gas stations—one nearby and one 15 minutes away that is 15 percent cheaper. That choice, between saving money or saving time, carries with it opportunity costs to the driver of lost money or time that could be spent on other things.

### Expensive gas station nearby

The extra money paid by using this gas station is the opportunity cost. That money might have been used for something else.

**Cheaper gas station farther away**

The time it takes to drive to the cheaper gas station is the opportunity cost. That time might have been used for something else.

"Money is all about opportunity. Every time you spend it on one thing, you're not going to be able to spend it on something else."

Dan Ariely, Israeli-American behavioral economist, Think Forward Initiative (2017)

## PRODUCTION POSSIBILITY FRONTIER

Plotted as a curve on a graph, the production possibility frontier (PPF) is a way for economists to study opportunity costs. The graph takes two goods and explores what different quantities of each can be produced to make the best use of a finite amount of resources. The curve illustrates the required trade-off—the opportunity cost—between the goods to optimize their production. In the graph below, points B, D, and C show the ideal outputs for apples and pears given the level of resources, such as labor, land, and expertise. Here, increased pear production means fewer apples, while fewer pears means more apples. At point A, resources are not being used efficiently, while point X can only be achieved with greater resources, such as more space for cultivation, a bigger workforce, or improved machinery. Using the PPF, the grower could work out what might be the best mix of fruit production—point D.

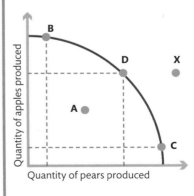

# Specialization

In most countries, people earn money by specializing in particular tasks, such as nursing, making furniture, or growing fruit. This is known as the division of labor.

## Single-minded

In some parts of the world, it is still possible for people to do everything themselves, from growing food to building a home. However, nearly everywhere, people and businesses specialize, and labor is divided; some people grow food, some process it, some sell it, and so on.

The 18th-century economist Adam Smith placed this division of labor at the heart of economics, arguing that economies grow as people specialize and make exchanges to receive everything else they need. The more specialized workers and businesses become, he argued, the more markets expand and the

greater the returns on investments. At the same time, goods become cheaper and wages rise.

## Divisions in society

Economist Karl Marx (1818–1883) criticized Smith's model, arguing that specialization and the division of labor lead to dissatisfaction, as

## Divide and conquer

In modern economies, people and businesses specialize and trade to meet their multiple needs by buying from other specialists. A supermarket may provide everything a person needs in one place, but the store itself receives its products from a huge array of specialists. In modern economies, the work of different specialists can be classified into four sectors: primary, secondary, tertiary, and quaternary.

**Specialists**
People who specialize become masters of their crafts. Practice also enables them to increase output.

FRUIT GROWER

BAKER

DAIRY FARMER

**Shared goods**
Due to trade, each person gets the full range of goods and services that they need by buying from other specialists.

workers are pushed into dull, repetitive jobs (see pp.132–133). Others, too, argued that specialization creates hierarchies as some people become managers and others laborers. Nevertheless, labor division is now the norm in modern economies.

Specialization can be both microeconomic and macroeconomic. Individuals can specialize in skills, and entire countries can focus on sectors in which they have an advantage (see pp.158–159).

## PROS AND CONS OF SPECIALIZATION

Although people and institutions have become more specialized over time, there are both pros and cons to specialization.

### Pros

> **People can focus** on doing what they do best.

> **Increased skill** helps workers make things better and faster.

> **It enables** mass production and economies of scale (see pp.50–51).

> **Production** is more efficient, which reduces scarcity.

### Cons

> **Repetitive** and unvaried tasks can be boring.

> **People become** less self-sufficient and therefore more vulnerable when trade is interrupted.

> **Work forces** become inflexible and unable to respond to changing demands.

## ECONOMIC SECTORS

### Primary
Workers in the primary sector—which includes mining, farming, fishing, and forestry—extract raw materials from the Earth.

### Secondary
In the secondary sector, raw materials are turned into manufactured goods. These include vital utilities, such as electricity and fuel.

### Tertiary
The tertiary, or service, sector includes the retail, financial, IT, communication, hospitality, tourism, and entertainment industries.

### Quaternary
The quaternary sector includes the public sector, education, the knowledge economy, and scientific research and development.

## CASE STUDY

### Growing apples

Division of labor has become global in scope. A good example of how a single product can be the work of numerous specialists is Apple's famous smartphone, the iPhone. Surprisingly, it is not strictly an American product, but involves many specialists working across the world. The designers are mostly in the US, as well as a small proportion of the company's sales team. However, the phone itself is assembled by workers in China, Vietnam, and India using parts that are made in other far-flung countries. The phone's case, its screen, and its processors are built in South Korea, Japan, Germany, and various other countries—and even these parts contain elements that are the work of teams of other specialists.

# Factors of production

Economies produce goods and services using four different categories of "resource": land, labor, capital, and enterprise. These resources are known collectively as "factors of production."

## Building blocks

Factors of production are the building blocks of every economy. The output of goods and services depends entirely on the inputs of the factors of production. However, these factors must be available in the right quantity, at the right time, and at the right price. Each is—to some degree—of limited availability, and it is this scarcity that gives them their economic value, and so creates a demand. A "free good" is something that has unlimited availability, such as air or seawater, so it is not a factor of production. However, in reality, very few things are really without cost—for example, one of the costs of economic growth may be air pollution.

## Basic ingredients

In order to produce goods and services, an economy draws on all four factors of production: land (the Earth and its natural resources); labor (the work that people do to make things); capital (the tools, machines, buildings, and other equipment that people use to make other things); and enterprise (the skill and ideas that are needed to set up and maintain a production process).

### Land
All of the Earth's natural resources. Some of these will eventually run out, but others are renewable.

### Labor
All of the people who are available to work. Different sections of the labor force have different skills.

### Capital
The equipment, offices, vehicles, factories, and schools that the labor force uses.

In fact, some economists argue that economies should be judged according to the extent to which they damage or help the environment (see pp.142–143).

### "New" factors

Land, labor, and capital were identified as the key factors of production by early economic thinkers such as Adam Smith and Karl Marx (see pp.132–133). Because many people now live and work entirely within urban areas, land has become less important, and labor and capital have become more so. Enterprise is a fourth factor that was added more recently.

Some economists argue that other factors should now be considered. These include knowledge, or "human capital" (the skill or ability of workers), which they claim is distinct from labor or enterprise; or technology, which can actually be used to replace other factors—for example, the use of robots to replace workers on a production line.

### OWNERSHIP

Control of the factors of production is the key to wealth. People who own a lot of land or capital are invariably wealthy, and their wealth can give them control over additional factors of production. In the capitalist system, business owners and investors control most of the factors of production, whereas in socialist systems, the government may have greater control.

## "It is preferable to regard labor ... as the sole factor of production."

John Maynard Keynes, *The General Theory of Employment, Interest and Money* (1936)

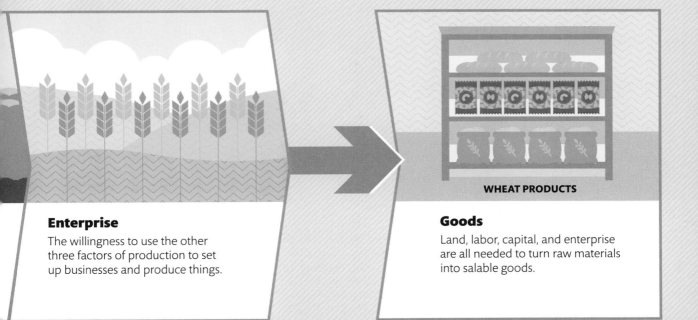

**WHEAT PRODUCTS**

### Enterprise

The willingness to use the other three factors of production to set up businesses and produce things.

### Goods

Land, labor, capital, and enterprise are all needed to turn raw materials into salable goods.

# Transaction costs

A transaction cost is any expense incurred in making an economic trade. In key circumstances, transaction costs can have large effects on economic decisions.

## The price of trading

Most economic models assume that trading is costless, so they focus on other aspects of the market instead. However, there are three ways in which using the market is costly: search costs are incurred by looking for someone to trade with; dealing costs are the costs of making a deal; and enforcement costs are the costs of ensuring that parties to a deal honor its terms. These expenses may be fees paid to agents to work on a principal's behalf to make a deal, or to lawyers for drawing up contracts, or simply the time spent looking for someone to do business with.

Britsh economist Ronald Coase (1910–2013) pointed out that it is partly due to transaction costs that people form companies—because companies have departments that deal with those costs, which frees everyone else to perform their own specialized tasks. Although this is more economical than individuals trading by themselves, a company's transaction costs become part of its bureaucracy and may eventually generate inefficiencies that have to be dealt with—usually by closing or selling a business unit. In this way, transaction costs can create cycles in which companies form, split, and restructure themselves.

## Restructuring markets

Transaction costs can change the structure of markets. For example, insurance companies traditionally only did business via brokers, but a fall in the cost of technology reduced transaction costs and led to the industry selling directly to consumers. However, that made it harder for consumers to compare prices, which created an opportunity for entrepreneurs to set up online recommendation sites that served as a new type of intermediary in the industry. This reduced search costs for consumers and increased sales for insurance companies.

## TRANSACTION COSTS ECONOMICS

In contrast to traditional economics, Transaction Costs Economics (TCE) offers an alternative approach for analyzing trades.

### Traditional approach

❯ **The deal** is analyzed in terms of the goods and services that are traded.

❯ **The firm** is simply a producer.

❯ **Property rights**—laws about who owns which resources—are a given.

❯ **Goal focus** asserts that maximizing profit is the single goal of efficiency.

❯ **Behavior** of all parties is completely rational.

### Transactional approach

❯ **The deal** is analyzed in terms of the transaction itself.

❯ **The firm** is an organizational structure.

❯ **Property rights** can raise transaction costs, which reduces efficiency.

❯ **Goal focus** asserts that all goals have limitations.

❯ **Behavior** follows "bounded rationality"—choosing a satisfactory outcome instead of a perfect one.

## The division of costs

All firms incur transaction costs. They pay external transaction agents to provide goods or services that they cannot supply themselves. Some costs are internal because firms provide their own functions. Sometimes firms expand outside their original area of expertise to supply additional goods or services in house. While some services, such as accounting, are done internally by most firms, small firms may choose to employ an external accountant.

## External transaction costs

These costs are incurred when bringing in materials to make a product or when getting it to market.

 **Finance and legal** Bank charges, currency exchange, legal fees, insurance

 **Marketing** Market research, branding, advertising campaigns, promotions

 **Transportation** Packaging, moving goods, warehousing

 **Retail** Identifying retail customers, negotiating deals, samples, trade fairs, discounts

## AN INTERNET REVOLUTION

Introduced in the 1990s, the internet has lowered transaction costs and made markets more competitive, which benefits both producers and consumers. The internet has particularly lowered the cost of searching for information. Services such as online shopping and banking also lower transaction costs and match sellers with buyers more efficiently (see p.79). The internet has made it easier for small businesses to compete and reach more customers, although the dominance of larger players has also increased.

**COMPANY A**

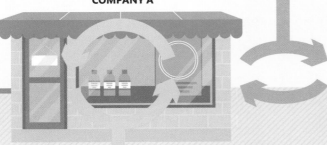

**COMPANY B**

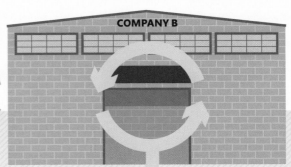

## Internal transaction costs

These costs are incurred entirely within an organization.

 **Planning** Research and development, focus testing, design, trials, prototypes, samples

 **Administration** Strategy, budgeting, forecasting, reporting, management

 **Human resources** Recruitment, training, looking after workers, resolving disputes

 **After-sales service** Technical support, warranties, feedback, loyalty programs

# Property rights

**Markets are places in which people exchange property—which can be goods or assets—but they can only run smoothly if property rights are clearly defined and regulated.**

## Types of property

Property rights are central to economics because they are the basis of all exchanges in the market. A person can only sell something that is theirs to sell, and for this reason, it is vital that who owns what is clearly defined. Property can range from "tangible" (physical) goods, such as houses and cars, to "intangible" goods, such as shares, bonds, and other financial assets (see pp.188–189). It also includes intellectual property, such as music, patents, and copyrighted ideas.

Property rights are usually guaranteed by laws that are laid down by the state. These define what ownership is, state the limits of what owners can do with their property, and exclude others from using it.

For example, house owners may be allowed to alter their houses as they wish so long as they conform with government planning laws, conservation laws, and building regulations. They may also be entitled to protect their property from trespassers.

## Safe trading

Property rights also determine how resources are allocated across the whole population. They give the owner the right to do what they want with their

## Tangible property

The most familiar type of property is tangible property, which includes land, housing, and personal possessions. In legal terms, there are three main kinds of tangible property: private, public, and common property. Most economies contain a mixture of all three, from privately owned houses to commonly owned land and publicly owned hospitals.

### PROPERTY AND PRICE

Individual property rights underpin competitive, capitalist economies. Property owners are effectively competitors, because only one person or business can own a particular property. Each transaction in the marketplace is therefore a transaction between a property owner and a property buyer. The price at which a property changes hands depends on how much it is valued by the owner and the buyer—which is usually the highest price that the buyer is willing to pay.

### PRIVATE PROPERTY

Property owned by individuals and businesses is protected by private property rights. These rights also give the owner the right to exclude others from using their property without permission.

property, which includes altering it, selling it, or renting it. If these rights are properly regulated, individuals can trade with confidence. If not, exchanges become problematic, and one person can accuse another person of buying, selling, or holding property illegally.

## "Freedom and property rights are inseparable. You can't have one without the other."

George Washington, president of the United States (1789–1797)

## UNOWNED RESOURCES

Bad property rules can have disastrous environmental consequences. In a phenomenon known as the "tragedy of the commons" (see pp.68–69), natural resources, such as walking land and fishing areas, are more likely to be misused if they are neither privately owned nor administered by the state. In other words, if no one owns the land, it is much more likely to be spoiled.

**SPOILED WATERS**

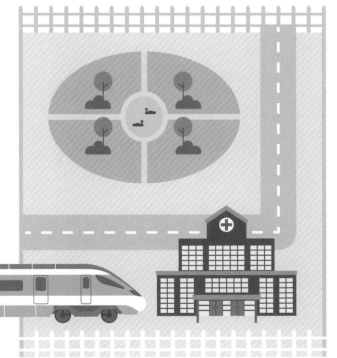

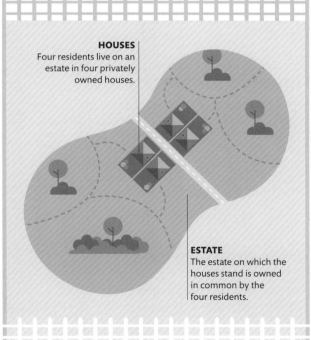

**HOUSES**
Four residents live on an estate in four privately owned houses.

**ESTATE**
The estate on which the houses stand is owned in common by the four residents.

## PUBLIC PROPERTY

State-owned properties, such as national parks, are known as "public properties" because they are administered by the government on behalf of the people, who pay for them with their taxes.

## COMMON PROPERTY

Property that is owned and administered by many people is known as common property. Such property includes fishing areas, grazing land, and common walking land.

# Economic systems

Economies are either based on free market (capitalist) or command (communist) systems. Most markets have evolved to be a mixture of these two structures.

## Capitalism vs. communism

In the 19th century, industrial nations such as the US allowed those who owned land, factories, and machinery to run their businesses with minimal government regulation. This was called *"laissez faire"* ("allow to do") and later, capitalism. In the last century, neoliberal economists (see pp.140–141) argued for even less government control, believing that only a market free from regulation is efficient. In communist economies, such as those in the Soviet Union and the People's Republic of China, governments had total control.

By the end of the 20th century, most communist states were beginning to open up their markets, while capitalist states intervened more, providing welfare and utilities to deal with inequality and other problems that seemed common with capitalism. Most economies today combine capitalism with a level of state control.

# 58.3%

was the share of **state spending in France's GDP**

International Monetary Fund (2022)

## The three systems

The economic systems are command economy (communism), free market (capitalism), and mixed (for example, democratic socialism). Most economies today are a mixture of privately owned businesses alongside state control of natural resources such as water and forests.

## COMMAND ECONOMY

In a command—or planned—economy, systems are centrally planned. The government sets production targets, controls distribution, and decides wages. Most industry is state owned, and competition is limited or nonexistent. With profits removed and wages set, there is often little incentive to improve.

**GOVERNMENT**

**PRIMARY SECTOR**    **MANUFACTURING**    **RETAIL**

**What to produce**
The government decides what will be produced, removing all choice.

**How to produce**
Production methods are set by the government, but producers may have some choice.

**Who to produce for**
The government controls where goods and services can be bought.

*Pros*
The focus is on goods and services for all. The aim is to overcome market failures, minimize inequality, put social welfare before profit, and avoid mass unemployment.

*Cons*
Governments may respond slowly to changing preferences, leading to shortages and surpluses. Free choice is restricted. Without profit, incentive is reduced.

## FREE MARKET ECONOMY

In free market, capitalist economies, the market and the pursuit of self-interest control the economy and stimulate competition. Businesses and consumers interact freely, dictating demand and supply. This influences prices and how resources are allocated, a process referred to as the "pricing mechanism."

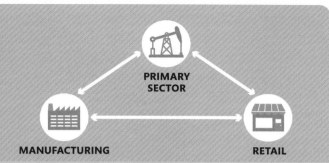

**PRIMARY SECTOR**
**MANUFACTURING**
**RETAIL**

**What to produce**
Consumer preference establishes demand for particular products.

**How to produce**
Producers decide how they can profit by meeting consumer demands.

**Who to produce for**
Prices set by producers decide who can afford their products and services.

**Pros**
Competition boosts quality and lowers prices. Profit motives reduce waste, supply and demand allocates resources efficiently, and people enjoy more choice.

**Cons**
Free markets underprovide public goods (see p.36), and inequality is prevalent. Monopolies—where a firm has little competition—develop easily, and prices fluctuate.

## MIXED ECONOMY

A mixed economy combines free markets and government control. Individuals and businesses own private property and have freedom over their economic choices. At the same time, the government supports the economy to achieve social, political, and national agendas.

**GOVERNMENT**
**MANUFACTURING**
**PRIMARY SECTOR**
**RETAIL**

**What to produce**
Production is directed by consumer preferences and government decisions.

**How to produce**
Producers decide how they can profit, but the government plays a part in steering production.

**Who to produce for**
Prices set by producers together with government preferences determine where products go.

**Pros**
Consumers and businesses pursue their own choices. Governments intervene, giving financial support to address market failures and aid industry and agriculture.

**Cons**
Social welfare creates a high tax burden. Interventions can upset supply-demand mechanisms (see pp.44–45), and the system is open to lobbying for self-interest.

# Markets

For economists, the word "market" can describe a physical location, such as a local market, where people exchange goods and services, but it also refers to the entire theoretical system of buying and selling.

### The marketplace

A marketplace provides the means for people to get a hold of the goods and services they want from producers and for producers to sell their wares, usually in exchange for money. Marketplaces have existed since ancient times, when humans first began to trade (see pp.182–183), and ruins of these can be seen today at the Forum in Rome, Italy, and the Agora in Athens, Greece, among other places. Many towns and cities still have busy marketplaces today, where all kinds of produce is bought and sold.

But for economists, the "market" is much more than an open-air space with market stalls—it applies to every area of the economy in which exchanges take place. It might be a website or app where craft products or clothes are sold, or it might not have any physical reality at all—the "job market," for example, is simply the overall process by which job seekers and employers find each other. There are countless different kinds of market these days, both physical and virtual, and they arise whenever people want goods or services that others can provide.

### Choice and competition

The concept of the market is at the heart of all economics, and what all markets have in common is choice and competition, selling and buying, and supply and demand (see pp.44–45). Competition is key, allowing the price to be set in response to the balance between supply and demand: if demand is high and supplies are short, prices rise; if demand is low and supplies are high, prices drop. This is the key mechanism of the market.

## Features of a market

A market can be small, with just a few stalls or a parade of shops, or it can be large, such as a shopping mall. But the biggest marketplaces of all are online: half a trillion US dollars of sales flows through Amazon each year. Every market, whether it is physical or virtual, has a number of defining features.

### Arena

The arena is where deals are done. This can be a physical marketplace that both sellers and buyers travel to or an online location where transactions can take place.

### Buyers and sellers

Every market needs sellers and buyers who are willing to come together to make a deal. Sellers and buyers can be individuals or large organizations.

## THE WHEAT MARKET

Wheat provides a fifth of the world's food. As the population grows, demand for wheat rises, pushing prices higher, but there are many other factors that can affect its price. For example, a price spike in 1996 was largely caused by bad weather, and a larger spike in 2008 was driven by rising oil prices—which increased the demand for crops to feed biofuels. However, prices can drop with events such as good harvests.

GLOBAL PRICE OF WHEAT

1996 Grain price shock

2008 Oil price rise

US DOLLARS PER METRIC TON

YEAR

"**The** market economy is very good at wealth creation but not perfect at all about wealth distribution."

Jonathan Sacks, British rabbi and philosopher, *Markets and Morals* (1998)

**Goods**

A market must have goods or services to be bought and sold—either a single commodity, such as wheat in the global wheat market, or many commodities, such as produce at a local market.

**Prices**

In every market, commodities have prices. These can vary depending on competition and the balance between supply and demand. Understanding this is at the heart of economics.

**Competition**

Markets must have more than one buyer and seller. Alternative sellers allow the buyer to choose, and this creates the competition that controls prices.

# How markets fail

Market failure is caused by supply and demand being unbalanced—in other words, by markets either failing to provide what people want or providing too much or too little of it.

## Unwanted consequences

Many economists used to believe that the most efficient way of allocating resources in society was to give free rein to the forces of supply and demand (see pp.44–45)—in other words, for governments to stay out of the market and leave producers to produce what people want and let prices settle at their natural level. However, even the most ardent advocates of the free-market economy (see pp.126–127) now accept that there are many situations in which leaving the market to operate by itself leads to unwanted consequences. These consequences include what economists call "externalities" (see pp.66–67), which are costs paid by people who are not involved in either producing or consuming a good or service. A dramatic example of such a cost is the rise in global temperatures caused by industries polluting the atmosphere with greenhouse gases.

Today, economists recognize that there are many causes of market failure (see below)—the problem is deciding how to deal with them. Some argue that government intervention is necessary, while others believe that they can be solved by the market itself—and some argue that they cannot be solved at all.

## Ways of failing

There are eight key ways in which a market may fail. These range from the existence of negative and positive externalities to the fact that some goods are unpopular even though they benefit consumers, while others are commercially viable even though they are harmful to consumers and may be very expensive.

### Negative externalities

Damages incurred by third parties. For example, a producer may sell a chemical to a consumer, neither of whom pays for the pollution the chemical causes (see pp.66–67).

### Positive externalities

Benefits enjoyed by third parties. For example, a teacher may educate a student who then shares what they have learned with other students for free.

### Information failure

Negative consequences that result from consumers or producers not having all of the information about a good or service (see pp.72–73).

### Public goods

Tax-funded goods or services, such as street lighting, that people benefit from even if they fail to pay their taxes (see pp.70–71).

## CASE STUDY

### Environmental damage

A potentially catastrophic example of market failure is the environmental damage caused by industries that burn fossil fuels. To address this, many governments have introduced carbon taxes to reduce carbon emissions (see p.67). However, carbon taxes do not necessarily reduce pollution. Some industries simply raise their prices to cover the extra cost, or buy the "right to pollute" with schemes such as carbon trading, which enable them to produce emissions so long as they fund emission-reduction schemes in other industries.

## IS POVERTY A MARKET FAILURE?

Poverty is increasing across the world, and the gap between the rich and the poor is widening (see pp.122–123). Many economists argue this is a market failure, not only because of the misery it causes, but because it goes against market logic: producers have to sell the goods they produce, but as the majority of people get poorer, the market for those goods can only shrink. Some economists advocate government intervention to correct this failure—for example, by taxing the wealthy or providing subsidies to those living in poverty.

> "Climate change is a result of the greatest market failure the world has seen."
>
> Nicholas Stern, British economist, *Stern Review on the Economics of Climate Change* (2006), commissioned by the UK Treasury

## Monopolies

Firms (see pp.58–59) or groups of firms (see pp.60–61) that dominate a market to such an extent that new firms are unable to start up in the market.

## Factor immobility

When a factor of production (see pp.26–27), such as labor, is unable to move easily from one region of an economy to another.

## Merit goods

Goods or services, such as renewable energy and education, that have a beneficial effect on the consumer but may be underused if left to the forces of supply and demand.

## Demerit goods

Goods or services, such as tobacco and gambling, that can have a harmful effect on the consumer and may be overused if left to the forces of supply and demand.

# MICROECONOMICS

Microeconomics is a branch of economics that deals with the decisions of individual "agents"—consumers and firms. It examines how they behave and exchange within different types of markets.

# The consumer

Microeconomics revolves around consumers—as their needs and demands power markets. Because consumers are a key driving force in the economy, economists try to understand their buying behaviors.

## Universal market driver

Every individual is a consumer (a buyer of goods or services), and what consumers spend is by far the largest share of a country's gross domestic product (GDP)—the total value of its products and services (see pp.88–89). The valuations made by consumers of what they need drive the demand side of a market. The problem for economists is that consumers are people and therefore differ greatly in their outlook on products and services. To impose some understanding on consumer choice, economics relies on a simple set of assumptions about consumers—they know what they want, are consistent in their preferences, and aim for maximum utility—the value and enjoyment they get from the goods or services they choose to buy (see pp.16–17). From this, economists draw up a simple behavioral model—the demand curve (see right).

## Demand behaviors

Economists say that consumers faced with price changes react in two different ways while making sure they still get the best utility. When prices rise,

# £361.3bn

## was spent by UK consumers in the second quarter of 2019—the highest amount on record

www.tradingeconomics.com (2023)

## Consumer reactions

In economics, the consumer is modeled as a rational individual, optimizing their consumption decisions to maximize utility. Two different behaviors—income effect and substitution effect—drive the consumer's reactions to price changes.

### Rational consumer

Given that a consumer cannot control prices and has a limit to their budget, they want to achieve as much utility as possible in their purchase choices.

### Price changes

Rising or falling prices signal to a consumer that they have to revise their spending decisions. They will change their level of consumption to get the best possible utility.

consumers can afford less, so they either buy less as a whole or buy the same amount of some products or services but fewer of others. This is the "income effect." Alternatively, consumers replace one product or service with something cheaper to maintain their level of utility. This is the "substitution effect."

The two behaviors apply to most markets, but there are exceptions. For example, in super-luxury markets such as for yachts, demand is fueled by the utility derived from showcasing one's ability to afford such extravagant goods.

## THE DEMAND CURVE

Plotting the relationship between the price charged for a good or service and the amount that consumers will buy creates a demand curve. The curve reflects the market norm that as the price of a particular good or service rises, the quantity demanded will fall—known as an inverse relationship. Conversely, the curve also shows that an increase in quantity will lead to a drop in price.

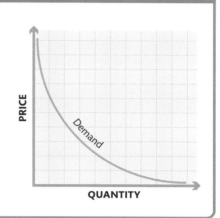

### Income effect

A price rise is equivalent to a fall in income because it leaves the consumer with less purchasing power. Conversely, a rise in income will encourage a consumer to buy more.

As purchasing power rises, consumers spend more

As purchasing power falls, consumers spend less

### Substitution effect

A consumer may switch to a cheaper product if prices rise, or a more expensive one if prices drop. Changes in demand will depend on the availability of substitutes.

As prices rise, consumers may not just buy less, but might switch to cheaper items

As prices drop, consumers may not just buy more, but might switch to more expensive items

## ✓ NEED TO KNOW

❯ **Consumer demand** What goods and services individuals want to buy and their willingness to pay a specific price for them.

❯ **Consumer spending** The total amount spent within an economy by individuals and households on goods and services for their own use and enjoyment.

❯ **Consumer price index (CPI)** A monthly measure of changes in prices—and a key measure of inflation (see pp.96–97). Also known as the retail price index (RPI), the figure is quoted as a percentage based on the average cost of a selection of popular goods and services.

❯ **Rational consumer** A model of an individual who makes purchase choices based on what is of most benefit to them in terms of usefulness and satisfaction.

# The firm

Firms make and sell the goods and services that consumers buy within an economy. A firm aims to make as much profit as possible based on decisions about investment, labor, price, and volume.

## The production balance

In economics, production is the function of firms—companies, institutions, and other groups of people that make and sell goods and services to consumers. The basic role of firms is to maximize profit—income after costs and expenses—by producing goods they can sell for more than it costs to make them.

To reach a level of production that can create a profit, firms use a combination of labor (workers) and capital (tools, machinery, buildings, financial investment, and other assets), which is called a technology (the means to produce the goods). To achieve the optimum quantity of goods or services, a firm increases its output up to the point where the cost of producing one

extra unit (the marginal cost) would exceed the income from that unit (the marginal revenue).

The decision over how much to produce is affected also by shifts in consumer demand (see pp.40–41) or the effect of price changes on the supply of goods. A firm's revenue depends on both the price of the good and its utility—the value consumers place on that good and

## The route to profit

A firm is assumed to want to maximize its profits. It will do so by choosing the best level of output given its technology and the cost of its inputs. The inputs will be capital (all assets, including financial investment) and labor (workers).

### PRODUCTION FACTORS

In theory, a firm maximizes its profits by simply producing as much as it can at the lowest cost. However, to get to this point, a firm has to balance certain factors—particularly capital and labor—then take account of the level of consumer demand and pricing within its industry to fine-tune its production estimates.

**INVESTING IN CAPITAL**
A firm invests money in the capital required to create its product.

**ALLOCATING LABOR**
A firm chooses labor levels based on the expected wage rate and labor output.

**PRODUCTION TECHNIQUES**
Combining labor and capital, a firm chooses a technology to make its product.

whether they can afford it. The more a firm can get for a good, the more likely it is to produce it.

## Influential actions

Although consumer demand largely drives market activity, changes in how firms act can also have an impact. For example, advances in production technology can reduce costs and make goods cheaper, while adverse factors—such as obsolete equipment or a scarcity of raw materials—could increase a firm's costs, decrease output, and raise prices.

## THE SUPPLY CURVE

The correlation between the price charged for a product and the total amount produced by firms within a particular industry creates a supply curve. It links the cost of producing one extra unit of a product to its price—the higher the price, the more the firms in the industry will be likely to produce. As a result, the curve slopes upward, indicating a positive relationship between price and quantity for producers.

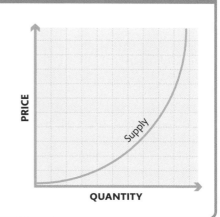

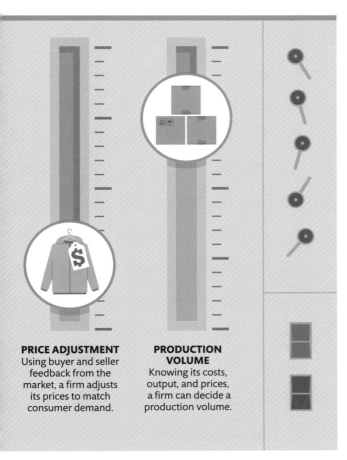

**PRICE ADJUSTMENT**
Using buyer and seller feedback from the market, a firm adjusts its prices to match consumer demand.

**PRODUCTION VOLUME**
Knowing its costs, output, and prices, a firm can decide a production volume.

## ✓ NEED TO KNOW

> **Marginal cost** The change in a firm's production cost caused by making one more unit.

> **Marginal revenue** The change in a firm's revenue from the sale of one more unit of product or service.

> **Productivity** A measure of a firm's efficiency that compares output against input for either labor or capital.

> **Price signal** A change in the market, such as a shortage of goods or change in consumer taste, that affects prices and indicates to a firm that it should review its level of output.

# 63.5%
of small businesses
in the US were
profitable in 2022

Guidant Financial, "Small Business Trends" (2022)

# Supply and demand

The supply and demand model explores the relationship between the selling and buying of goods and services. Its purpose is to help markets determine the best balance between prices and quantities.

## Following the curves

One of the simplest ways to understand economic activity in a market is to study how the amounts of goods or services (the supply) interact with what consumers want to buy (the demand). This basic model can be presented graphically using two "curves," often drawn as straight lines—one for demand, the other for supply—allowing economists to measure different market scenarios and how they affect prices and quantities of goods and services.

The "demand" curve follows the connection between price and quantity for a buyer. As the price for a product or service rises, fewer consumers want to buy, so demand for quantity falls—and the curve slopes downward. The "supply" curve shows the relationship between price and production for all the firms in the market. As the price goes up, existing firms start to supply more of a product or service, or additional firms decide to enter the market. That makes the supply curve slope upward.

The point where the two curves cross is called the equilibrium. Here, consumer demand exactly matches the quantity of the product or service, with no shortage or excess in supply. At an equilibrium, there is no call for prices or supplies of goods and services to change.

Once the point of equilibrium is known, it is possible to investigate what happens when something changes one of the factors determining supply or demand.

## Shifts in demand

When the factor that changes is something other than price, a parallel shift in both curves shows the effect of that change. For instance, a rise in consumer income will increase demand, making that curve shift right, while a rise in production costs for all firms in an industry may reduce supply, making that curve shift left. This creates a new equilibrium where supply and demand are in balance.

---

## SUPPLY AND DEMAND MODEL

The basic model is based on price being the key factor that affects both supply and demand. Other factors, such as fashion, quality, and new technology, are not taken into account. This clarifies the effects of price change on any one curve. If another factor is added, the model reflects this by shifting the demand or supply curve to find a new equilibrium.

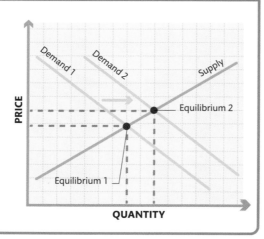

**26% was the overall drop in UK consumer demand during the COVID-19 crisis in 2020**

McKinsey Global Institute, "The consumer demand recovery and lasting effects of COVID-19" (2021)

# Tracking price fluctuations

A state of equilibrium does not mean that prices will remain stable. In practice, the equilibrium between price and quantity can fluctuate quite widely. However, every price swing can be accounted for by economic conditions, which will show up in shifts of the supply and demand curves. If there are price fluctuations, the market will attempt to compensate by adjusting supply and demand to bring them back into equilibrium.

 **NEED TO KNOW**

❯ **The law of demand** As the price of a good or service increases, the quantity demanded for that good or service will fall. Conversely, as the price decreases, the quantity demanded increases.

❯ **The law of supply** An increase in the price of a good or service leads to an increase in the quantity supplied, while a decrease in price results in a lower quantity produced.

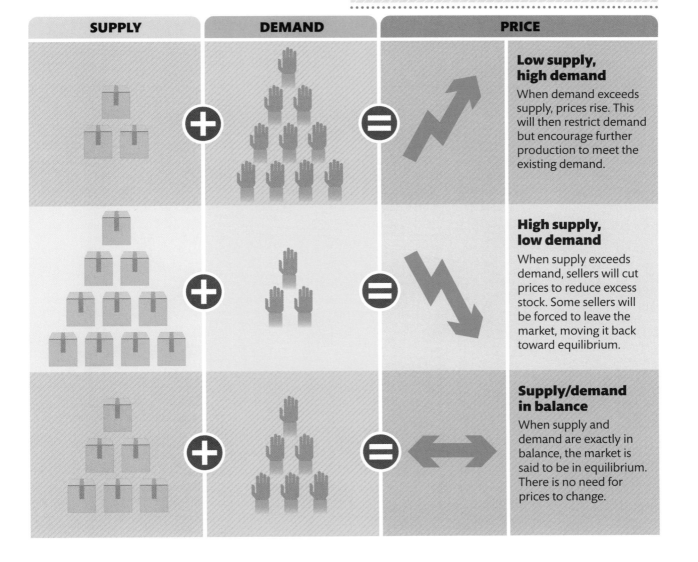

| SUPPLY | DEMAND | PRICE |
|---|---|---|

**Low supply, high demand**

When demand exceeds supply, prices rise. This will then restrict demand but encourage further production to meet the existing demand.

**High supply, low demand**

When supply exceeds demand, sellers will cut prices to reduce excess stock. Some sellers will be forced to leave the market, moving it back toward equilibrium.

**Supply/demand in balance**

When supply and demand are exactly in balance, the market is said to be in equilibrium. There is no need for prices to change.

# Elasticity

In economics, the term "elasticity" is most commonly used to describe the relationship between price and demand—specifically, the sensitivity of demand to changes in price.

## Elasticity of demand

The price elasticity of demand is a measure of the extent to which the demand for goods is affected by a change in their price. A good is "price elastic" if consumers buy less of it when its price rises, but "price inelastic" if its price has little effect on demand. A "perfectly elastic" good, such as insulin, is one that consumers will buy at any price (if they can), whereas a "perfectly inelastic" good, such as gold, is one that is valued for having a fixed price at any time. A "relatively elastic" good (such as a bicycle) is one that consumers will pay a little more for if necessary, whereas a "relatively inelastic" good (such as salt) is one that people will pay a lot more for, but only up to a point. Some goods (such as fruit) are "unit elastic," which means that an increase in their price produces a proportional decrease in demand.

## Measuring elasticity

Price elasticity is measured by finding the percentage change in the demand for a good after it has

## Types of elasticity

There are several types of elasticity calculated in economics. Some, for instance, relate to substitution between goods or factors of production (see pp.26–27). The most commonly used, however, are the own-price, cross-price, and income elasticities of demand.

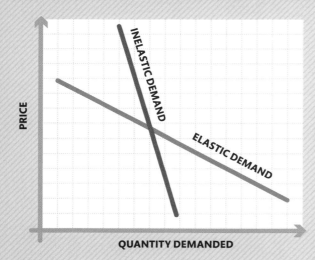

### Own-price elasticity

This is measures the responsiveness of the demand for a good to changes in its price. A high responsiveness indicates elastic demand, while a low responsiveness indicates inelastic demand.

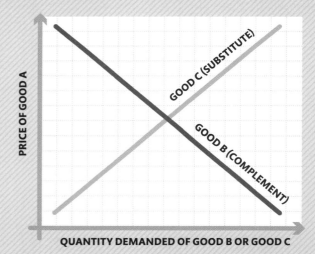

### Cross-price elasticity

This measures how the demand for one good responds to the price of another. If cost-price elasticity is positive, the goods are substitutes, and if the cost-price elasticity is negative, the goods are complementary (used together).

increased in price by 1 percent. A good that has an elasticity of -3, for example, is one that loses 3 percent of its demand after a 1 percent increase in price. While decreases in demand usually follow price rises, not all price elasticities are negative. For example, some luxury items become more popular the more expensive they become.

## "Price is what you pay; value is what you get."

Warren Buffett, American businessman, 2008 Berkshire Hathaway Inc. shareholder letter

## BUSINESS STRATEGIES

Just as different goods have different price elasticities, so the industries that produce them have different business strategies. A firm that produces price-inelastic goods, such as oil and gas, can hold consumers for ransom by charging them high prices. On the other hand, a firm that produces price-elastic goods, such as candy, can undercut its rivals by lowering its prices.

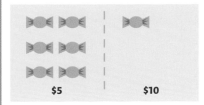

**Elastic**
The demand for candy is elastic; it varies depending on price.

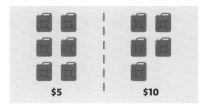

**Inelastic**
The demand for gasoline is inelastic; it stays fairly constant.

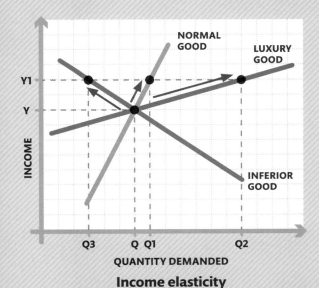

### Income elasticity
This measures how sensitive quantity demanded (Q) for a good is to a change in consumer income (Y). It can be used to tell if a good is inferior, normal, or a luxury (see right).

**Inferior goods**
Goods that decrease in demand as consumer income increases—for example, used clothing.

**Normal goods**
The demand for normal goods, such as gas, is only slighted affected by income changes.

**Luxury goods**
Goods that significantly increase in demand as income rises—for example, jewelry.

# Production costs

The expenses incurred by a firm as it manufactures a product or provides a service are known as its "production costs." These include the price of raw materials and workers' wages.

## Total, average, and marginal costs

Firms face a variety of costs, from the cost of renting premises to the ongoing cost of items such as software and machinery. Economists categorize these costs according to which are production-related and which are not. Two key distinctions are between total costs and average and marginal costs. The total cost is the cost of producing a complete batch of goods, whereas the average cost is the cost of producing a single unit (the total cost divided by the number of goods in a batch). Firms use the average cost to calculate markups (the amount they can charge for goods after production costs have been accounted for) and economies of scale (the amount they need to increase production by to attain maximum efficiency). The marginal cost is the amount it costs to increase production by a single unit. This figure is used in setting levels of production—the optimal level is

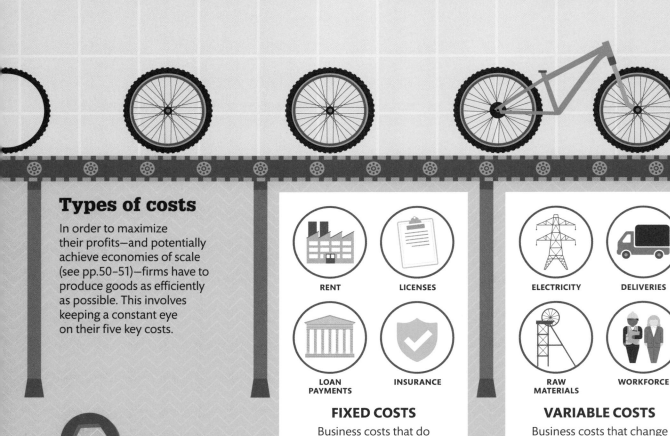

## Types of costs

In order to maximize their profits—and potentially achieve economies of scale (see pp.50–51)—firms have to produce goods as efficiently as possible. This involves keeping a constant eye on their five key costs.

RENT

LICENSES

LOAN PAYMENTS

INSURANCE

ELECTRICITY

DELIVERIES

RAW MATERIALS

WORKFORCE

**FIXED COSTS**
Business costs that do not change as production levels rise or fall.

**VARIABLE COSTS**
Business costs that change depending on the level of production.

when the marginal revenue received from selling a single unit is equal to the marginal cost of making it (see pp.42–43).

## Fixed and variable costs

Another key distinction is between fixed and variable costs. Fixed costs are costs that do not depend on the level of production. For example, a manufacturing firm incurs the cost of building or hiring a factory before a single production cost. Variable costs, on the other hand, depend entirely on how many units are produced—which in turn depends on how much raw material and labor goes into the process. The more the firm produces, the higher the variable cost.

### CHANGING WITH THE MARKET

If the cost of manufacturing a product becomes too high, a firm can try to increase sales by marketing the product for a new demographic. Alternatively, it can try to reduce its production costs. This could involve substituting existing materials and methods for cheaper alternatives. However, a firm that focuses too much on cost savings risks compromising the quality of its product. If neither option works, the firm may have to close—either temporarily (until the market changes) or permanently.

**TOTAL COSTS**

The total cost of producing a batch of goods.

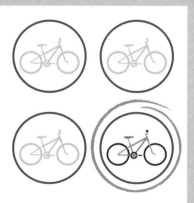

**AVERAGE COSTS**

The total cost of producing a batch of goods divided by the number of goods produced.

**MARGINAL COSTS**

The increase in total production costs incurred by producing one additional unit of a good.

# Economies of scale and scope

**As firms get bigger, they can benefit from economies of scale and scope—spreading their costs over more goods or services. This means greater efficiency, higher profits, and potentially lower prices.**

## Making more from more

Economies of scale are savings made by a firm when it produces more goods or offers more services. As it does so, the fixed proportion of its costs—such as rent, insurance, and advertising—is absorbed across more goods or services, and average overall costs fall. As a result, the firm will operate more efficiently, creating greater profits for itself and lower prices for consumers. It will also encourage efficiencies in competing firms.

Most processes involved in the making of products, including machine operation and the supply of raw materials, are usually performed more cheaply in bulk. Similarly, the selling of services can become more efficient and profitable by the scaling up of tools such as computer software and data gathering. Also, external but beneficial factors outside a firm's control, such as new suppliers of raw materials or improved transportation links, can create greater efficiencies. Eventually, issues that arise from the expansion of production or services, such as hiring too many

## Economies of scale

If a technology firm increases its computer production, it will benefit from economies of scale. Although some costs rise in line with output, some costs stay at the same level. More efficient use of the firm's resources and greater quantities of product lead to higher profits.

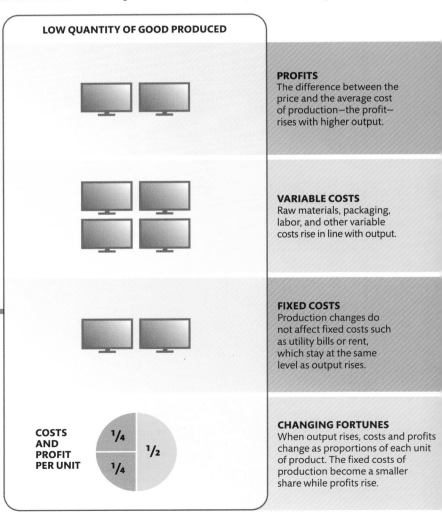

**LOW QUANTITY OF GOOD PRODUCED**

COSTS AND PROFIT PER UNIT

¼  ½  ¼

**PROFITS**
The difference between the price and the average cost of production—the profit—rises with higher output.

**VARIABLE COSTS**
Raw materials, packaging, labor, and other variable costs rise in line with output.

**FIXED COSTS**
Production changes do not affect fixed costs such as utility bills or rent, which stay at the same level as output rises.

**CHANGING FORTUNES**
When output rises, costs and profits change as proportions of each unit of product. The fixed costs of production become a smaller share while profits rise.

employees or overinvestment in machinery, will lead to rising unit costs. At this point, economies of scale become diseconomies of scale.

## Sharing resources

Firms can make further cost savings through economies of scope—the sharing of materials or processes across two or more products or services. For example, a shirt-maker could use fabric offcuts for other garments, or an airline might use its planes to carry cargo as well as passengers. Economies of scope are also achieved when firms merge and share their resources.

## AVERAGE COST CURVE

The effect of increased production on costs is illustrated by the average cost curve. Economies of scale are highest when the average cost—the total cost of making a product divided by the numbers produced—is at its lowest. This point is known as the minimum efficient scale (MES).

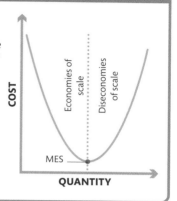

COST

Economies of scale

Diseconomies of scale

MES

QUANTITY

### HIGH QUANTITY OF GOOD PRODUCED

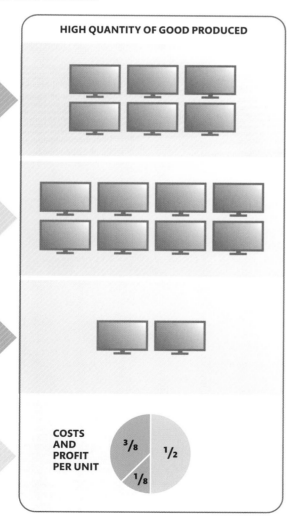

COSTS AND PROFIT PER UNIT

3/8  1/2  1/8

"Economies of scale ....
If we didn't have them,
we'd still be living in tents
and eating buffalo."

Jamie Dimon, American banker, *The New York Times* (2010)

## ECONOMIES OF SCOPE

A firm that makes different but related products—such as a manufacturer of technology goods—can achieve lower costs and increased efficiencies by using more of the same components across the product range. This is an economy of scope.

# Markets and industries

**To understand how markets and industries work, economists study both supply and demand—in other words, what industries are able to provide and what consumers want.**

## Firms and consumers

Industries are groups of firms (see pp.42–43) who provide particular goods or services for consumers (see pp.40–41), whose collective demand makes up their markets. A "market" is therefore both a place, either real or virtual, in which goods or services can be transacted (see pp.34–35) and the demand that makes such transactions possible. Particular industries, such as film production or aerospace, can be grouped into categories known as "sectors," which include entertainment, manufacturing, and retail.

Defining an industry enables meaningful comparisons to be made between the performance, costs, revenues, or efficiency of firms within it, even if they don't share the same geographical

## Market demand and industry supply

Markets and industries are the two sides of any exchange that takes place between buyers and sellers. The test for defining them involves identifying all the close substitutes for their goods or services—whether an item can be easily replaced by another to fulfill either demand or supply.

**CONSUMERS**

**CLOSE SUBSTITUTES**
Yellow and green tennis balls are close substitutes. A rise in the price of one will cause an increase in demand for the other.

**NONSUBSTITUTES**
Demand for bicycles and for fish is not related. A rise in the price of one will have little effect on demand for the other.

### A MARKET

A group of consumers who want to buy the same thing make up a market. Their combined preferences create demand. If what they want is too expensive, consumers in a market are more likely to switch to an alternative if it is a close substitute.

### MARKET DEMAND

Whether goods or services are in the same market depends on how likely a consumer would be to buy something as an alternative if their first choice weren't available.

location. This makes it possible, for example, to analyze the output of the Korean electronics industry in the Argentinian market.

## Supply and demand trends

Once markets and industries are identified, they are useful for analyzing how prices and quantities of products and services adjust depending on supply and demand (see pp.44–45).

Analyzing a market involves finding out where the opportunities are for selling a product or service— possibly to increase a market share—which requires detailed research into consumer preferences, product pricing, and product positioning. Analyzing an industry is more straightforward and involves examining the key players and trends in that industry.

### MONOPOLY MARKETS

The definition of a market is important when it comes to identifying monopolies, and it can be a matter of legal dispute. In a monopoly, one supplier has a dominant share of the market, which can be detrimental to free competition and consumers (see pp.58–59). Regulators may use legal powers to prevent or break up a monopoly, but first they need a precise definition of the relevant market. The "hypothetical monopolist test" starts with a broad definition of a market, then eliminates all goods or services that are not "close enough" substitutes until what remains must be the relevant market.

Sales take place where market demand and industry supply match at the right price.

**CLOSE SUBSTITUTES**
The output of a cornfield could be used for food or to make oil. Therefore, sweetcorn and corn oil fuel are substitutes in supply.

**NONSUBSTITUTES**
Clothes and computers are not substitutes in supply. Changing operations to produce computers instead of clothes is complex.

**FIRMS**

**AN INDUSTRY**
Firms with the same core activity make up an industry. Industries are classified according to various codes, such as the North American Industry Classification System (NAICS code) or the Statistical Classification of Economic Activities in the European Community (Code NACE).

**INDUSTRY SUPPLY**
An industry is defined by its activity. Whether goods or services are in the same industry depends on how easy it is to switch from producing one item to the other.

# Labor markets

In labor markets, firms demand and people supply work. The interaction between these two parties determines wage and employment levels within an economy.

## Demand and supply

Looking at labor as a kind of market helps economists think about issues surrounding work, wages, and employment. Supply and demand are approached in a different way to markets selling goods and services as firms provide the demand with their need for labor, which individuals supply. The price charged is now the wage level of the employees instead of the cost of goods and services; the quantity is represented by the total number of people employed, as opposed to the amount of goods and services that are provided.

## Labor and wages

Because labor is used to make goods, which are sold on markets, labor is both an output (or service) for workers and an input (the element needed to produce goods) for firms. As a result, labor costs are a factor in the prices consumers pay, with a rise in labor costs often leading to a rise in the price of goods. Firms are therefore eager to understand the increase in output they get for each extra worker's

## Every worker counts

The "marginal product of labor" (MPL) measures changes in output with the latest additional worker. Typically, output goes up with an extra employee; however, returns can start to diminish. Here, for example, the amount of apples and available ladders are fixed, so the fourth worker adds little value. By calculating MPL, firms can monitor when additional staff reduce profitability.

## Total output

Plotting the total output of apple pickers against the number of workers shows how the output for each worker gradually reduces. This is called "diminishing returns to labor."

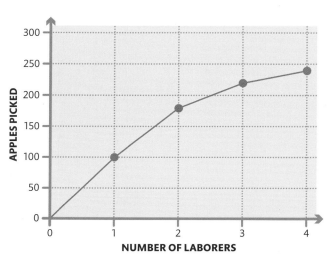

1

100 APPLES

**MARGINAL PRODUCT OF LABOR = 100**

input. Referred to as the "marginal product of labor" (see below), this can drive long-term trends in wages. This is because when productivity ceases to rise with new workers, wages and employment levels are revaluated.

## Sticky markets

Labor markets can also be "sticky" (see p.105), where wages adjust slowly to economic changes. For example, in downturns, employers often reduce work forces instead of lowering wages as workers and trade unions resist wage cuts. Instead, shorter, or zero-hour, contracts may be introduced and employee benefits reduced.

(see p.105)

### ✓ NEED TO KNOW

> **Labor productivity** The overall output produced by a group of workers in a given time period.
> **Marginal product of labor** The change to output that results from adding an additional worker.
> **Minimum wage** The lowest legal amount that employers must pay their workers per hour.
> **Trade unions** Groups of employees who collectively work to get the price for their members, where negotiating individually reduces bargaining power.

**MARGINAL PRODUCT OF LABOR = 80**

180 APPLES

**MARGINAL PRODUCT OF LABOR = 40**

220 APPLES

**MARGINAL PRODUCT OF LABOR = 20**

240 APPLES

# "Perfect" competition

The term "perfect" competition describes a market that is as competitive as possible—in which consumers get the best possible value for money but firms can find it challenging to make a profit.

## Limited competition

A perfectly competitive market is a theoretical model of a market that is the opposite of a monopoly (see pp.58–59). Although no such market exists, the model is useful for understanding many real-life markets that are almost perfectly competitive—"perfect" in the sense of having clearly defined limits (see below).

A perfectly competitive market is one that has numerous buyers and numerous firms that compete with each other to sell identical or near-identical products. Currency exchange and agricultural markets are good examples of these, because both trade the same interchangeable products. It is also one that is costless for sellers to

## A perfect marketplace

Independent fast-food outlets are good examples of firms that exist in a state of near-perfect competition. They sell effectively interchangeable products for returns that only just keep them in business while providing customers with the cheapest meals possible.

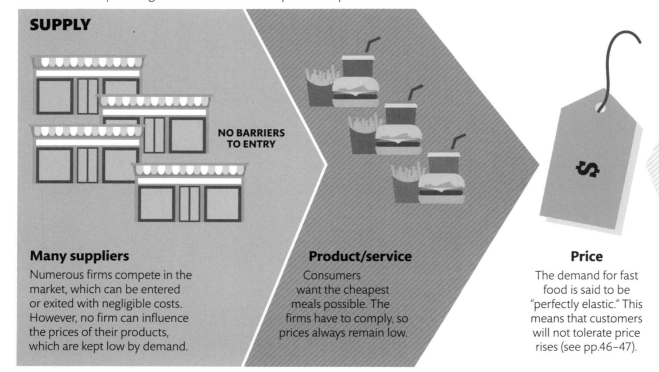

**SUPPLY**

**NO BARRIERS TO ENTRY**

### Many suppliers
Numerous firms compete in the market, which can be entered or exited with negligible costs. However, no firm can influence the prices of their products, which are kept low by demand.

### Product/service
Consumers want the cheapest meals possible. The firms have to comply, so prices always remain low.

### Price
The demand for fast food is said to be "perfectly elastic." This means that customers will not tolerate price rises (see pp.46–47).

enter or exit—in other words, one that takes little or no initial investment to enter and can be left without paying fees, such as redundancy costs. Finally, it is one in which both buyers and sellers have complete information about the product. In such a market, firms make no profit at all after their costs have been accounted for.

## Price-takers

In perfectly competitive markets, firms do not have control over the prices they charge for their goods, but instead are happy to take the market price as given. Economists call such firms "price-takers": if they raise their prices, they will lose their sales to rivals, and if they lower them, they will gain their rivals' sales until they are forced to raise their prices back to the market price. Because there are many sellers in such markets, no firm accounts for more than a tiny slice of the market. Plus, because they make no profits, they are unable to invest in their businesses, so they can never improve their products.

## ENTRY COSTS

Obstacles that prevent new firms from entering a market are known as "entry costs." These can include the amount of money that firms need to spend in order to set up their businesses—which may require machinery, retail outlets, and warehouse space—and the loyalty that customers already have to similar brands. Exit costs are the expenses that firms incur when they decide to leave a market.

## DEMAND

### Many consumers

There is a huge number of consumers in the fast-food market. No one individual can influence market prices.

## "... pure competition turns out not to be the ideal but a departure from it."

Edward Chamberlain, American economist, "Product Heterogeneity and Public Policy," *The American Economic Review, Vol. 40, No. 2* (1950)

## INNOVATION

Because firms in perfectly competitive markets make no profit, they are unable to innovate, as doing so costs money. This means that while customers benefit from cheap prices, the product or service they receive never changes or improves.

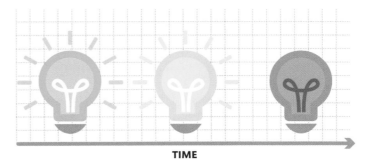

**TIME**

# Monopolies

A monopoly is a market structure with a single, dominant supplier and little or no competition. This lack of competition can make the market perform less well than alternative models.

## Limited competition

Monopolies usually occur in markets that are difficult for new competitors to enter and where products or services have no substitutes, meaning consumers cannot choose an alternative.

Monopolies can arise from numerous scenarios. Where a larger firm benefits from extreme economies of scale (see pp.50–51), this may make it impossible for smaller rivals to compete. They are forced out of the market, thereby creating a monopoly. A firm with a unique technical or other advantage can cause a monopoly. Sometimes, these advantages are legalized as patents or trademarks, or a government may grant a firm the sole right to trade in a particular market. A "natural monopoly" occurs in a free market where only one product or service is available because the high barriers to entry make the activity economically viable only if one firm serves the whole market. For example, railway networks and some utilities are natural monopolies.

## A monopoly-dominated market

In conventional economics, a rational firm is assumed to want to maximize its profits. In this example, a single supplier sells water in a market where the water supply has been privatized. Because water is a natural monopoly, the privatized market is dominated by a monopoly.

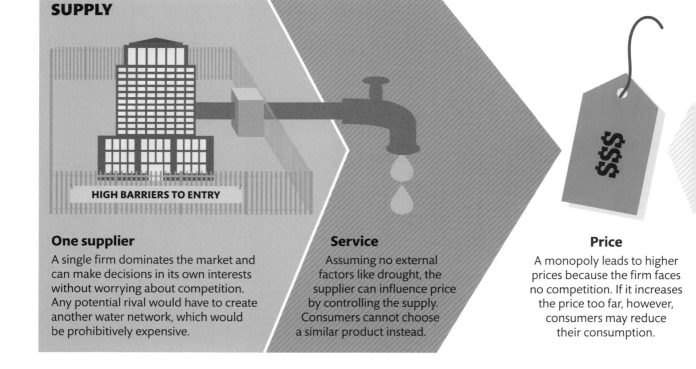

**SUPPLY**

**HIGH BARRIERS TO ENTRY**

### One supplier

A single firm dominates the market and can make decisions in its own interests without worrying about competition. Any potential rival would have to create another water network, which would be prohibitively expensive.

### Service

Assuming no external factors like drought, the supplier can influence price by controlling the supply. Consumers cannot choose a similar product instead.

### Price

A monopoly leads to higher prices because the firm faces no competition. If it increases the price too far, however, consumers may reduce their consumption.

# "Monopoly is a terrible thing— unless you have one."

Rupert Murdoch, Australian-born media entrepreneur, quoted by
Andrew Neil in *Full Disclosure* (1996)

Monopolies bring stability and can give firms the confidence to invest. However, they can also lead to low-quality goods. Unscrupulous firms can fix prices at a higher-than-reasonable level or artificially restrict supply. This causes a "deadweight loss to society"— that is where everyone misses out on the benefit of the extra output.

## Legal regulations

There are certain legal restrictions on monopolies to enable free competition. Antitrust laws in the US, such as the Sherman and Clayton Acts, and competition laws in the European Union (EU), such as Article 102 TFEU, may even allow governments to break up monopolies (see pp.64–65).

## CASE STUDY

### Google Shopping

By 2010, Google had a monopoly in the EU for internet searching, and it promoted the shopping links of companies that paid over those that did not. This distorted the market and led to higher prices for consumers. After a lengthy legal process, Google was fined more than $1.7 billion (€2 billion) and ordered to change its practices.

## DEMAND

### Many consumers

There is high demand for water, but no individual can influence the price. People must buy at the set price or reduce their water consumption.

# MERGERS AND ACQUISITIONS

A firm can increase its market share and benefit from economies of scale by integrating with another existing company. Two firms can join together as equals (a merger), or one firm can take over another (an acquisition).

## Vertical integration

This type of integration occurs when one firm merges with or acquires another that fulfills a different role in its supply chain. For example, a manufacturer could join forces with the firm that processes its raw materials (backward integration), with the firm that distributes its finished products (forward integration), or both.

| EXTRACTOR OF RAW MATERIALS |
| PROCESSOR OF RAW MATERIALS |
| MANUFACTURER |
| DISTRIBUTOR |
| RETAILER |

## Horizontal integration

This type of integration occurs when one company merges with a competitor. Such activity is often legally regulated to avoid the creation of a monopoly.

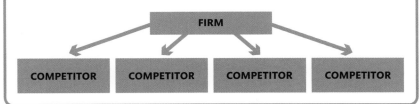

# Oligopoly

**An oligopoly is a market in which there are only a small number of firms that may work together in order to maintain their dominance and to deter any rivals from entering the market.**

## Restricted markets

Oligopolies are very common, occurring in markets as varied as those that specialize in everyday supermarket items and those that produce high-end electrical goods. A striking feature of an oligopoly is that firms operating within one rarely change their prices in response to changes in demand. This is due to the fact that such firms interact strategically and make decisions based on their beliefs about what their rivals are doing instead of what they think consumers might prefer.

Oligopolies exist for two reasons. First, due to economies of scale (see pp.50–51), it is cheaper for large firms to make products than smaller firms simply because they make a larger number of products, so they can spread their costs out more efficiently. For this reason, oligopolies tend to occur in industries that feature substantial economies of scale, such as the automobile, media, and pharmaceutical industries. Second, firms already in the

## An oligopoly market

An oligopoly, such as the pharmaceutical industry, has several key characteristics. First, it is has both high entry and exit barriers. Second, the strategic behavior of its firms leads to fewer price changes. Last, products may not necessarily be differentiated.

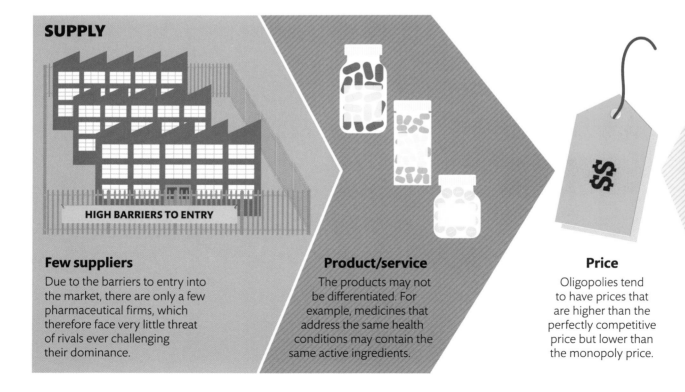

**SUPPLY**

**HIGH BARRIERS TO ENTRY**

### Few suppliers

Due to the barriers to entry into the market, there are only a few pharmaceutical firms, which therefore face very little threat of rivals ever challenging their dominance.

### Product/service

The products may not be differentiated. For example, medicines that address the same health conditions may contain the same active ingredients.

### Price

Oligopolies tend to have prices that are higher than the perfectly competitive price but lower than the monopoly price.

# "Oligopoly ... is saved only by its incompetence."

John Kenneth Galbraith, American economist, *The New Industrial State* (1967)

industry are rarely threatened by newcomers because the cost of entry into such industries is high—requiring, for example, a huge investment in machinery and factory space. As a result, prices in oligopolies tend to be higher than they would be in a perfectly competitive market but lower than they would be in a monopoly.

Because only a small number of firms control an oligopoly, anything that one firm does affects the others, which means that it is in all of their interests that they cooperate to some degree. However, antitrust laws exist to penalize firms that act as cartels—that is, groups of companies that make it impossible for new firms to enter the market.

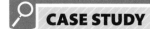

## CASE STUDY

### The automobile industry

Automobile manufacturing is a good example of an oligopoly. In the US, the market is dominated by Ford, Chrysler, and General Motors, whereas globally there are only 10 or so key manufacturers, including Honda, Renault-Nissan-Mitsubishi, Toyota, and the Volkswagen Group. Each company has its own niche in the market.

## DEMAND

### Many consumers

There are many consumers, but none may ever be in a position to influence the price.

## CARTELS

A cartel is a group of firms that have agreed to limit production or raise prices or even to share customers and markets for their common benefit. Although cartels were banned after World War II, cartel-like practices are still common. For example, Virgin and British Airways were prosecuted in 2006 for fixing the prices of transatlantic flights.

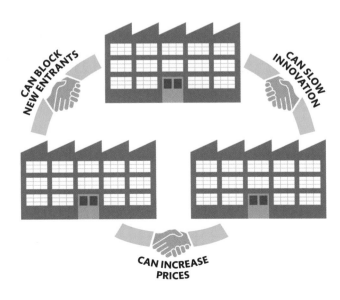

CAN BLOCK NEW ENTRANTS

CAN SLOW INNOVATION

CAN INCREASE PRICES

# Monopolistic competition

**When several firms provide products and services that are similar but not perfect substitutes for each other, they exist in what economists call monopolistic competition.**

## A crowded market

A monopolistically competitive market is one in which there are numerous firms selling similar products or services to numerous consumers, who are happy to change brands if one is sold at a lower price than another. Common real-world examples include the competition that exists between hotel chains and between companies that produce similar kinds of household cleaning products. In all cases, there is a slight difference between the products or services, but not enough to deter customers from spending their money elsewhere if necessary. To maintain their customers' loyalty, therefore, such firms spend a lot of money on

## Monopolistic competition in a market

A television channel occupies a niche in the market and makes a profit for as long as it can prevent competitors from entering the market and taking its place. If it cannot differentiate itself successfully, then a rival channel will do just that.

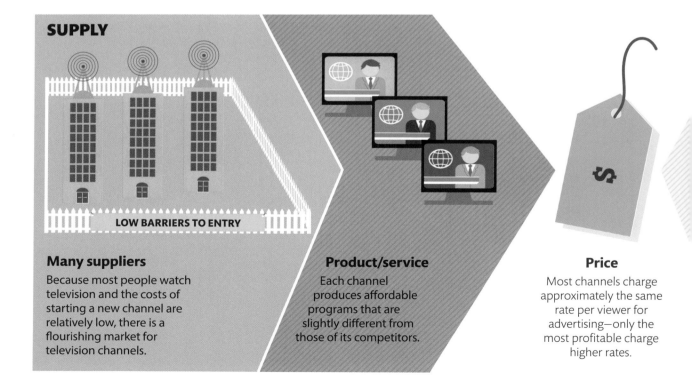

**SUPPLY**

**LOW BARRIERS TO ENTRY**

**Many suppliers**
Because most people watch television and the costs of starting a new channel are relatively low, there is a flourishing market for television channels.

**Product/service**
Each channel produces affordable programs that are slightly different from those of its competitors.

**Price**
Most channels charge approximately the same rate per viewer for advertising—only the most profitable charge higher rates.

branding and marketing, which can make the difference between the success or failure of their products or services.

## The long and short run

In monopolistic competition, firms are free to set the price of their product or service. However, due to the high level of competition, demand for their product or service will be highly elastic—in other words, will increase or decrease sharply depending on whether they lower or raise its price—so they must keep its price within a certain boundary. As a result of this, other firms may feel emboldened to enter the market, which in turn forces the existing firms to differentiate their products even further.

In the long run, companies in imperfect competition must keep investing in their products in order to keep them distinct. This can mean that they innovate and produce something unique, such as a more environmentally friendly version of a product that is already on the market.

> "The misery of being exploited by capitalists is nothing compared to the misery of not being exploited at all."
>
> Joan Robinson, *Economic Philosophy* (1962)

## DEMAND

### Many consumers

Demand remains high so long as channels keep their prices low and differentiate the kinds of programs they produce.

## PRODUCT DIFFERENTIATION

Monopolistically competitive firms face a dilemma: unless they differentiate their products from those of their rivals, they face more competition and make lower profits. However, if they differentiate too much, they risk no longer being in the market they want to be in—and possibly enter one that is too upmarket for the products they offer.

### Price

Firms in monopolistic competition tend to charge approximately the same amount for their products. This is because there is little flexibility in the price that customers are willing to pay.

### Quality

If a firm differentiates its product by lowering or increasing its quality, it can end up producing something that is either not good enough or too expensive for its intended customers.

### Marketing

Differentiating a product by giving it a distinctive brand and marketing it well is expensive. However, the expense can be greatly outmatched by the increase in the product's sales.

# Antitrust laws

When firms occupy a dominant market position, competition is reduced and consumers will lose out. Antitrust (or competition) laws apply economics to deal with the worst cases of consumer loss.

## A three-pronged approach

Market monopolies occur when several firms come together to dominate their field, therefore restricting the competitive nature of business that keeps prices low and quality high. In this way, monopolies can harm consumers from an economic point of view. Most governments have brought in laws to try to prevent these monopolistic practices—known as "trusts"—to ensure that markets remain fair and competitive.

The antitrust regulations are designed to address three problem areas. The first is the formation of cartels (see pp.60–61)—almost all such collusion is now illegal, and those firms found guilty of it will suffer heavy fines. The second is the abuse of monopoly. A firm in a dominant position is likely to set higher prices—again to the detriment of consumers. As a result, laws such as Article 102 in the European Union (EU) and the Sherman Act in the US make certain classes of behavior illegal if they can be shown to cause such harm to consumers. The final area these measures are designed to tackle is the overly concentrated market power that can accompany mergers and acquisitions (see pp.58–59). Nowadays, merger-approval laws exist to prevent such market control.

## Preserving competition

The legislation, known as "trust busting," aims to lower prices and increase production, as well as increase the degree of producer innovation and consumer choice. However, charges in this area can be tricky to prove, and because such large sums of money are involved, investigations are often strongly contested and can take a long time to complete. There is also some disagreement over whether the laws are sufficient to protect consumers.

## CASE STUDY

### Microsoft

In 1998, an antitrust case was brought against Microsoft, which was investigated in both the US and Europe. Microsoft's wrongdoing was to bundle its browser Internet Explorer with its operating system Windows. This gave it advantages over other firms, particularly its main competitor, Netscape. Microsoft was ruled to have "tied" its product with the intention of monopolizing the personal computer market. The company was fined more than $1.1 million (€1 billion) in Europe alone.

# $100m
## is the biggest fine a firm can face in the US for breaking antitrust laws

The Sherman Act, fourth amendment (2004)

# How the legislation works

Here, Article 102 of the Treaty on the Functioning of the European Union is used as an example, though these principles are broadly accepted throughout the world. This law relates to Abuse of a Dominant Position (behaving in an anticompetitive manner while also having a dominant share of the market).

**Limiting supply**
If, for instance, a firm has a key piece of intellectual property, it cannot refuse to license that property to a competitor.

**Excessively high pricing**
Firms have an incentive to set their prices too high, which harms consumers. This article aims to prevent that.

**Applying dissimilar trading conditions**
A firm must treat everyone in the same way. It cannot, for example, give rebates to favored customers.

**Requiring supplementary sales in order to buy a product**
"Tying," as it's known—making the sale of one product conditional on buying another—is illegal.

**Punishments**
If it is possible to change the behavior of the firm, then it may have to enter into a contract to say it will behave more fairly in the future. Firms may also be fined.

**Fragmentation**
If it is not possible to control the firm's behavior in these ways, fragmentation—the break-up of the monopoly—may be the only available action to regulators.

# External costs

Transactions between buyers and sellers often have consequences for third parties that have nothing to do with the transaction. These consequences are known as external costs, or externalities.

## Consumer choices

When a person pays for a product, it is often natural for them to assume that its price is an honest reflection of how much it cost the producer to make it. However, if making the product in some way affected a third party—whether positively or negatively—then the price no longer represents all of the value of the product. For example, if a factory buys a chemical from a supplier to make a product and pollution from the factory's production process contaminates a farmer's field, then the farmer, who was not involved in the transaction, incurs a negative cost—or negative

## Consequences for others

When individuals make transactions, they pay the private cost of their actions and usually receive private benefits. When an externality is present, the private cost does not take into account the costs paid or benefits enjoyed by other people.

### Positive externalities

A person who improves their home may generate benefits in excess of the cost of doing so. These could include:

❯ Increasing the property value of neighboring homes.

❯ Making the local area more visually attractive.

❯ Fostering a sense of pride in the local community.

externality—from the factory's purchase. At the other extreme, the whole of society benefits from having an educated population, so the construction of a school is a positive externality.

## Changing behavior

There are several ways of dealing with negative externalities. In the case of the farmer, the factory could pay him or her compensation for the losses caused by the pollution. Alternatively, the government could impose taxes to make polluting activity more expensive and to compensate those affected by it. If that fails, it could simply ban the polluting activity.

### Negative externalities

A homeowner may prove to be a liability to their neighbors. Negative externalities could include:

> Air pollution from fuels.
> Noise pollution from loud music.
> Congesting the road with vehicles.
> Leaving smelly trash out.

## CASE STUDY

### *Carbon taxes*

One way that governments combat climate change is by charging carbon taxes. These target industries that burn carbon and so release carbon dioxide (a greenhouse gas) into the atmosphere (see pp.142–143). Carbon taxes are based on the idea that a person incurs an external cost when they decide to buy a product or service that requires excessive amounts of carbon to produce or deliver—and that taxes can pay that extra cost. They are intended to encourage people to become less reliant on environmentally damaging industries.

## PIGOVIAN TAXES AND INCENTIVES

British economist Arthur Pigou (1877–1959) proposed that governments should tax transactions that create negative externalities—such as those caused by pollution. Today, taxes on carbon and sugar are examples of "Pigovian" taxes. However, governments can also subsidize firms that produce positive externalities—for example, that produce little or no pollution when manufacturing their products.

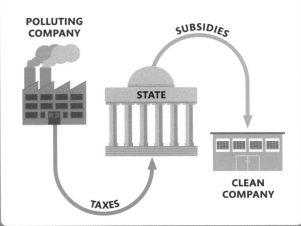

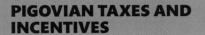

# Tragedy of the commons

The "tragedy of the commons" is a phrase that describes what often happens to natural resources when they are neither publicly nor privately owned: they lose their value by being overused.

## Private incentives

When individuals hold rights over resources—whether privately or communally—they have incentives to manage those resources sustainably. However, if those same resources are not owned by anyone, then anyone who wants to can exploit them. If too many individuals do this, then they will not be able to exploit the resources sustainably, leading to overuse and depletion of those resources. This tragedy of the commons can occur in many contexts. The resource might be agricultural land, a rainforest, an oil field, or even water, which has been the source of many conflicts throughout history. Likewise, fishing areas in the sea can be ruined if the numbers of fish within

## Grazing rights

A classic thought experiment illustrates the tragedy of the commons. The tragedy arises because there is a conflict between the individual interests of each farmer and what would be best for them collectively if they managed the land together.

### LOW USAGE

Each shepherd wants to maximize their use of the land for their sheep. But if they individually use it to a limited extent in order to preserve it for the future, then the land remains healthy.

### HIGH USAGE

If each shepherd uses the land as much as they want without any control, they all do well in the short term. However, the field becomes crowded and unhealthy from overuse.

them are not monitored and kept at sustainable levels (see box). In all cases where individual and collective incentives are not the same and people do not organize themselves to manage their resources, the collective loses.

## Avoiding tragedy

In places where rights over a resource are well established, institutions are often set up to safeguard the collective interest. For example, the Water Court of Valencia in Spain was established about 1,000 years ago to resolve conflicts over water rights and is still active today. Likewise, American economist Elinor Ostrom (1933–2012) studied African societies and discovered that many African peoples, particularly the Masai, safeguard their agricultural resources with well-defined sets of practices. These practices, which effectively ensure that common land is treated as if it were collectively owned, exemplify how best to ensure that a tragedy of the commons is avoided.

**CASE STUDY**

### Overfishing

Bluefin tuna fish is a highly prized culinary ingredient, so it commands a premium price. Because it is so popular, there is a high incentive for fishermen to catch it. As a consequence, stocks of bluefin tuna are in sharp decline, and several species of bluefin are even endangered.

"Freedom **in a** commons **brings** ruin to all."

Garrett Hardin, American ecologist, *The Tragedy of the Commons* (1968)

### RUINED LAND

If the shepherds continue to overuse the field, then the field's resources become depleted. Eventually, the land is stripped of grass and nutrients and can no longer be used for grazing.

## TRAGEDY OF THE ANTICOMMONS

The tragedy of the commons is a failure of cooperation. Equally tragic, however, is a situation in which too many people own a resource. For example, a group of people may refuse to sell their privately owned properties—possibly to make way for a community-level construction project—even though doing so would benefit not only their community, but themselves. In other words, although private property creates individual wealth, too much of it can be detrimental to the well-being of a community.

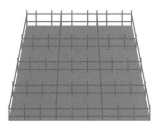

**PRIVATELY OWNED PROPERTIES**

# Public goods

Commodities or services that are available to everyone in society are known as public goods. These are typically administered by the government and funded by taxation.

## Defining public goods

In economics, there are many ways of classifying goods. One way of doing so is by asking two questions. First, is the good such that when one person consumes it, it does not prevent another person from doing so? Second, is the good such that it is impossible to prevent someone who has not paid for it from consuming it? If the answer to both questions is "Yes," then the good is a public good.

Public goods are mostly, but not always, provided by the state instead of by privately run businesses. Street lighting is a good example of why this is

## Types of goods

There a four main types of goods—private, common, club, and public—which in turn are either rivalrous or nonrivalrous in nature. The majority of goods are known as "economic goods," because they are scarce and have to be obtained through human effort. Much rarer are "free goods," such as air—these are abundantly available and take little or no human effort to obtain.

### Excludable
Excludable goods are goods that a person can be prevented from using if they do not pay for them.

### Rivalrous
Rivalrous goods are such that one person's use of them will affect another's. The marginal cost (see pp.48–49) of supplying the goods will therefore be greater than zero.

### Private goods
Private goods are excludable and rivalrous. They include common, everyday items such as books, hair dryers, and cars.

### Nonrivalrous
Nonrivalrous goods are such that one person's use of them does not affect another's. The marginal cost of supplying the goods will therefore be zero.

### Club goods
Club goods are excludable and nonrivalrous. They include goods such as cable TV, internet access in a coffee shop, and toll roads.

usually so. The light it produces is the same no matter how many people benefit from it, and it is impossible to prevent someone from benefiting from it without paying for it. Another source of public goods is philanthropy, such as when private land or property is free of charge.

## Restricting public goods

In some circumstances, public goods are made available without someone other than the consumer benefiting from them. A business might provide public goods, but only because doing so enables it to charge people for something else. The first lighthouses, for example, were often built to ensure safer landings at ports and increase the number of ships that used the ports, which also charged docking fees.

If public goods are restricted—such as when a road can only be accessed by drivers who pay a toll for it—they become "club goods." Another example of a club good is a television service that requires a subscription fee. Both provide an important service to the public, but at a financial cost.

### Nonexcludable
Nonexcludable goods are goods that a person cannot be prevented from using if they do not pay for them.

### Common goods
Common goods are rivalrous and nonexcludable. They can include roads, fish stocks, air, and water sources.

### Public goods
Public goods are nonexcludable and nonrivalrous. They can include schools, hospitals, police forces, national armies, and roads.

> "The more complex the civilization, the greater the number of public goods that needed to be provided."
>
> Martin Wolf, British journalist, *Financial Times* (2012)

## THE FREE-RIDER PROBLEM

People who use public goods without paying for them are known as "free riders." One way of dealing with free riders is to create exclusion mechanisms to keep them out. For example, streaming services that require subscriptions can be protected by passwords, which places a cost on the potential free rider, because stealing or hacking a password can take time and money. Applying such exclusion mechanisms to public goods effectively turns them into club goods.

# Asymmetric information

Information is "asymmetric" when one person or party knows more than another about a product or service during a transaction. Usually, it is the seller who knows more, but it can be the buyer.

## Lemon markets

Markets depend on good information to function. When one party in a transaction has more knowledge than the other, the differences, or asymmetries, can have a damaging effect on how the market works. In his book *The Market for Lemons* (1970), American economist George Akerlof (b. 1940) illustrates this concept through the example of the used car market. Sellers of second-hand cars have more information about the condition of their vehicles than potential buyers do and may offload low-quality cars (or "lemons") onto unsuspecting customers. Knowing that lemons exist in the market creates uncertainty for buyers, which in turn lowers the prices they are willing to pay for any second-hand car.

## Financial crash

In 2007–2008, the American financial market collapsed, triggering a worldwide recession (see pp.94–95). The disaster was largely caused by asymmetric information. Before 2007, banks extended cheap mortgages to consumers who, in many cases, were unaware that their mortgage rates would soon rise. The banks then pooled the mortgages and repackaged them as assets known as Collateralized Debt Obligations (CDOs). However, the investors who bought these CDOs were unaware that the mortgages they contained were "subprime"—in other words, had a high risk of not being repaid.

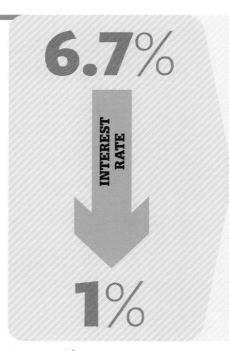

**BANK**

**HOME BUYERS**

**HOUSING**

> " ... the worst financial crisis in global history."
>
> Ben Bernanke, Chair of the Federal Reserve of the United States (2006–2014)

### Lowered interest rates

Between 2001 and 2004, to boost the American economy, the Federal Reserve (the US central bank) slashed interest rates. This encouraged people to take out loans and spend money.

### Housing boom

Taking advantage of low mortgage rates, banks sold properties to millions of people who would never have been able to buy a home otherwise. Housing prices soared.

Sellers with high-quality cars may then withdraw from the market due to the inability to secure fair prices, potentially leaving only low-quality, low-priced cars. If no trades occur, this market—known as a "lemon market"—could collapse.

## Adverse selection

In some transactions, one party can benefit from their superior knowledge—this is called adverse selection. Health insurance buyers are likely to know more about their own health than an insurer does, who, lacking sufficient risk information, might assume a greater risk and charge inflated premiums, putting off healthier, low-risk buyers. To avoid adverse selection, insurers use screening methods to assess each buyer's risk.

### MORAL HAZARD

Where a buyer or seller withholds information during a transaction or changes their behavior afterward—therefore exposing one side to greater risk—this is known as moral hazard. For instance, a householder might stop taking reasonable precautions after taking out home insurance.

**LOWER RISK TO THE INSURER**

**GREATER RISK TO THE INSURER**

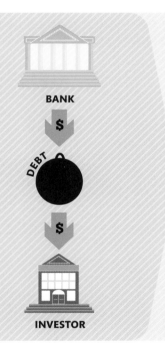

## Repackaged debt

The banks repackaged the mortgages as CDOs and sold them to investors—hiding the fact that many of the mortgages had an extremely high risk of not being repaid.

## Raised interest rates

Between the summers of 2004 and 2007, interest rates rose steadily, leaving millions unable to pay their mortgages. The CDOs became worthless, and investors lost their money.

## Bankruptcy

People unable to pay mortgages had their homes seized by the banks. From 2007, many banks in the US and beyond went bankrupt, and some came under government control.

# Incentivizing production

**Firms are incentivized to go into production when there is the possibility of future profits. If profits are uncertain, governments can use various tools to prompt production where necessary.**

## Uncertain profits

Typically, firms produce goods and services because they believe these will generate a profit. Sometimes, however, a product or service is needed by society but firms are reluctant to produce it if the profits are either too uncertain or likely to occur too far in the future to be able to count them as assets. In these cases, governments can incentivize firms to produce goods and services. They may do this, for example, to secure certain types of energy production (see box, opposite), support essential infrastructure, or incentivize the development of new technology. Incentives are either indirect—by introducing taxes or providing grants—or direct, providing financial incentives paid for by public taxes to spread the costs for firms (see below).

Direct incentives include supporting speculative research, for example, into a new technology. This can be done by awarding intellectual property rights (see pp.30–31) for a product, which give the holder a "limited duration monopoly" (exclusive rights to make and sell a product for a period of time) in return for incurring the costs of research and production for new inventions.

## Incentivizing solar power

Solar energy is becoming cheaper each year, but transforming energy systems to run on solar power involves high start-up costs. Several interventions can incentivize production of solar panels.

**GOVERNMENT**

**DIRECT INCENTIVES**

**INDIRECT INCENTIVES**

**POLLUTING FIRM**

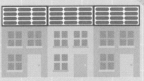

**HOUSEHOLDS**

### Taxing pollution

Carbon taxes make producing energy using polluting technologies more expensive, incentivizing firms to switch to new, less polluting sources of energy.

### Stimulating demand

Grants or cheap government loans for householders can subsidize the costs of installing solar panels and batteries so they increase demand for solar panels.

## Meeting upfront costs

Governments may need to meet upfront costs if these are prohibitive. Nuclear power stations, for instance, are costly to build, and it can be a decade or more before they generate revenue to pay for building expenses. Companies are unlikely to be able to raise capital from investors with such slow returns. They would therefore need a guaranteed subsidy even to begin the work on building a plant. In these cases, governments can provide direct loans (see box, right) or act as a guarantor to investor loans to enable production to go ahead.

> ## "Fiscal support can play a role in stimulating innovation ..."
> Ellen MacArthur Foundation

 **CASE STUDY**

### An energy transition

South Korea is a major fossil fuel importer because it lacks domestic coal and gas resources. To reduce its reliance on fossil fuels, it aims to generate 30 percent of the country's electricity through nuclear power by 2030. However, the costs involved in building and setting up a new nuclear plant account for nearly 60 percent of the plant's total lifetime costs, which means that making a profit is a faraway prospect. The South Korean government has therefore embarked on a major building program using direct subsidy and commitments to develop plants over the next 10 years to hit its target.

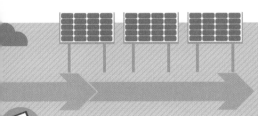

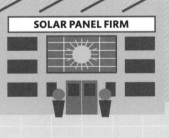

 **Tax credits**

Awarding tax credits allows manufacturers of new technologies to keep a greater proportion of their revenue, encouraging them to continue production despite high costs.

**Funding support**

Research and development (R & D) is often a long, expensive process with uncertain outcomes. Government funding for R & D can improve the quality of products and reduce manufacturing costs.

**Subsidies and grants**

Direct government subsidies, such as financial aid or loan guarantees, incentivize production. Grants do not need repaying but must be used for a defined purpose.

 **Regulatory support**

A supportive framework of rules and regulations can encourage the growth of new markets. Setting up good ground rules for the solar energy market while increasing existing regulations on the fossil fuel market can incentivize solar manufacturing.

# Time preference

Is it better to spend money now or invest it for the future? The answer depends on a concept known as "time preference," and a formula used by economists helps us understand how this works.

## Assessing the value of an investment

In economics, the decision on whether to spend now or save for later depends on "utility"—that is, the benefit or satisfaction derived from goods or services (see pp.16–17). An assessment is made on the utility gained by spending now or the potential utility gained by waiting to spend at a later date. An individual or company's preference for one of these levels of utility is referred to as a "time preference."

Deciding a time preference is complicated by the fact that the future is uncertain, so the value of something in the present is deemed greater than the promise of its potential future worth. Economists therefore use tools to compare present and future value.

## Equivalent values

A tool, or formula, called the "discount rate" is used to show present and future values together. Ideally, this captures both the time preference over the two periods and the risk of a future value not being realized. By multiplying future returns by a discount rate, they can be made equivalent to today's values, referred to as the "net present value" (NPV). If expected returns are too far in the future to assess—for example, the future financial impact of climate change and the benefits of intervention—finding a discount rate to compare the present and future accurately is not possible. In these cases, there are other methods of assessments governments can use.

## SETTING A DISCOUNT RATE

Discount rates are decided by working out the minimum acceptable rate of return on an investment over a set period of time. It takes into account all of the costs involved and the potential future risks, such as economic downturns, so a higher discount rate implies a greater risk and vice versa. For example, a discount rate of 20 percent might be applied to an investment in a start-up, while a lower discount rate of 5 percent might be suitable for less risky investments, such as in established firms.

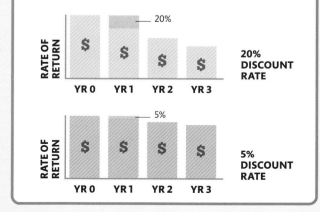

## Calculating NPV

To work out the net present value (NPV) of an investment, costs for the duration of the investment are taken into account and a discount rate is applied. This rate compares the current value of an investment with future returns. A decision can then be made as to whether it is worth going ahead with the investment.

"... present goods are always worth more than future goods of like kind and quality."

Frank Fetter, American economist,
*Economic Principles* (1915)

## 1. Should we invest?

A factory is considering investing in a machine that will cost $1,000 and return $500 a year over four years.

**INVESTMENT**
$1,000

**RETURN**

| Yr 1 | Yr 2 | Yr 3 | Yr4 |
|------|------|------|------|
| $500 | $500 | $500 | $500 |

## 2. Total investment return

Simply adding returns and subtracting the initial investment shows a profit of $1,000, but this does not give the whole picture.

$500
+ $500
+ $500
+ $500
- $1,000
= $1,000

## 3. Algebraic equation for NPV

To correct the projection, the zNPV formula for the future value of each of the returns is applied.

C = initial investment

$$\text{PRESENT VALUE} = \frac{C}{(1 + R)^T}$$

1 + R = discount rate used

T = number of years from the present

## 4. Applying a discount rate

Multiplying the future return by the formula gives a value in terms of today's money. Here, a discount rate of 20 percent (1.2) is assumed.

Yr 1

$$\frac{\$500}{(1.2)^1} = \$417$$

Present value of future return

Yr 2

$$\frac{\$500}{(1.2)^2} = \$347$$

Present value of future return

## 5. Time-adjusted returns

Completing the time adjustment stage for each year of the investment shows that its future value drops as time goes forward.

**INVESTMENT**
$1,000

**RETURN**

Today   Yr 1   Yr 2   Yr 3   Yr 4

$417 ← $500
$347 ← $417 ← $500
$289 ← $347 ← $417 ← $500
$241 ← $289 ← $347 ← $417 ← $500

## 6. Net present value

Adding the time-adjusted returns and subtracting the original investment shows a profit of $294. This is the net present value of the four-year investment.

$417
+ $347
+ $289
+ $241
- $1,000
= $294

294

# Economics of information

**Digitized information differs from other goods and services because it can be free to supply and consume. To make a profit, firms have to explore other ways to engage economically with consumers.**

## Information for free

Today, a substantial part of the economy revolves around trading information—or content—in the form of words, music, and video accessed on a computer, tablet, or smartphone. Once digitized, this information can be transmitted at zero cost, consumed repeatedly, and easily shared—often for free—from one person to another. The production cost and price differences between digital content and physical goods mean that content providers follow a different business model.

If each new consumer can digitally access content for free, there is no revenue (total income) for the provider, which has to find other ways to stay in business.

## Finding the profit

Firms typically monetize their digital content by running third-party advertising alongside it, whether on a website or app. Some firms adopt the freemium model, providing a free basic version of their service with the choice to pay for an ad-free experience.

## Physical vs. digital

All firms, including content producers, incur costs to supply goods (see pp.42–43). For physical goods, each new unit carries an extra cost—the "marginal cost"—with firms pricing their goods to cover this and make some profit. For digital goods, costs are high when a firm creates the first copy of its content but zero thereafter, allowing firms to offer almost limitless units and earn cost-free revenues.

# 92%
## of Americans accessed online content in 2023

Digital 2023: The United States of America

### Physical goods

A firm that offers information content in a physical form, such as a book or magazine, incurs a marginal cost for each unit, which includes production, labor, and distribution.

**MARGINAL COST = $2**

To avoid or restrict free access to content, many providers set up a digital barrier, or "hard paywall." A firm then invites the consumer to pay a subscription to read, watch, or listen to its content. Some firms offer a "soft paywall," which allows a consumer to receive some free content before having to pay for more.

Firms may also increase revenue by using the digital information, or data, they gather from their customers. Such data can help a firm improve efficiency, lower costs, and develop new products. Or a firm may offer data to another firm so it can market its products or services to new consumers. This has raised concerns over consumers' privacy, leading to some governments introducing rules to control data collection.

## CASE STUDY

### *The Wall Street Journal*

In the 1990s, as computer ownership rapidly increased, newspapers began to create websites where people could read articles for free. The idea was to attract new readers, but sales of newspapers began to fall. In 1997, American newspaper *The Wall Street Journal* was the first media outlet to introduce a "paywall," requiring readers to pay $50 a year to access digital versions of its articles. Although overall online use dropped, by April 1998, the newspaper had 200,000 digital subscribers, and other publications gradually followed suit.

## PLATFORMS

Information technology allows firms to operate not as producers of goods or services, but as online "platforms" that allow buyers and sellers to trade with each other. Platforms—via a website, app, or both—usually charge one side of the market and subsidize the other. For instance, an app store might charge app suppliers to sell on its platform but ask for no payment from users.

**PRODUCERS**
A platform allows producers to connect to potential buyers. Producers are charged a fee for this service.

**PLATFORMS**
Trading platforms take a fee from one side and subsidize the other by not making a charge. The fee tends to be taken from the producers, which boosts platform usage by consumers.

**CONSUMERS**
Customers pay for a product, with the platform's costs accounted for by the side of the market that pays a fee, usually the producers.

## Information goods

If a firm offers its content in a digital form to be viewed on a computer, tablet, or smartphone, there are no costs involved in presenting the information to the consumer once the content and the technology for supplying it have been created.

**MARGINAL COST = $0**

# Network effects

The power of networks—services and their users—has the ability to transform economies. Networks can affect markets directly and indirectly, creating value by, for example, simply increasing in size.

## The power of networks

Innovations in information technology, from the infrastructure of the internet to the rise of social media, have made connection cheaper and more available, boosting the power of networks. This has resulted in far-reaching economic changes, leading to the rise of new companies and the fall of several previously established ones. These changes all relate to the economics of networks, in particular to what economists refer to as "network effects."

## Types of network effects

There are two types of network effects. "Direct network effects" are benefits that arise from more people joining a network. This is also called a "same-side network effect" because a change in the number of customers causes an effect on the demand side of the market.

An "indirect network effect" happens when an increase in the number of users incentivizes suppliers to create more or better

## Direct network effects

In a telecommunications network, the benefit to an individual user depends on the number of people that user can communicate with. The more people the user can call, the greater the "utility"—the benefit or satisfaction derived (see pp.16–17), which, in turn, can increase demand.

NUMBER OF USERS $^2$
=
NETWORK VALUE

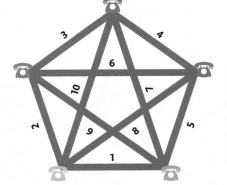

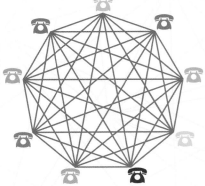

### 1. One connection
With just one connection, the user can make only one call. The resulting benefit to the user is low.

### 2. Unique connections
As the number of users grows, the benefit of being able to make and receive calls rises as possible connections in the network increase.

### 3. Developed network
Eventually, a high number of connections increases the value of the network, which approximates to the square of the number of users.

products. For example, the more subscribers a streaming service has, the more it will spend on content. Because the benefit occurs through a change in supply-side behavior, indirect network effects are also called "cross-side effects."

Combining network effects with digitalization means that the host company has continually falling average costs. In other words, the bigger a company becomes, the more money it makes without experiencing diseconomies of scale (see pp.50–51).

# 3bn
## monthly active users on Facebook in 2023

Meta, the parent company of Facebook (2023)

### ✓ NEED TO KNOW

❯ **Critical mass** The number of users required for a network effect to occur.

❯ **Congestion** A negative network effect where an excessive number of users slows the network down, reducing its efficiency.

❯ **Winner-takes-all markets** A market where there can only be one lead competitor.

## Indirect network effects

For a platform selling a product, it is the connection between users and the suppliers of a product that counts instead of the connection between individual users. In this illustration, the number of users affects revenue. In turn, the network invests in more suppliers and products.

**1. More users**
The network sits between producers and users. As a result, its job is to connect those users to producers. The more users a network has, the more it can connect to producers.

**2. More revenue**
This creates a cycle where the more users there are, the greater the revenue generated for the network.

**3. More suppliers**
The economic benefit leads the network to invest in more or higher-quality products.

**4. More variety**
Alternatively, it might choose to stock a wider variety of products through the network. This in turn attracts new users, increasing revenue income.

# MACROECONOMICS

The study of how whole economies perform, macroeconomics examines economic indicators like gross domestic product, growth, and unemployment and how they affect a nation or region—or even the world.

# The circular flow

An economic transaction is an exchange of resources between participants in a market. When a market is operating freely, these resources move in what is known as a "circular flow."

## Flowing in two directions

As money moves from consumers to producers, so goods and services move from producers to consumers. Likewise, when a government (or "state") raises money from citizens, it provides public services—such as state-funded hospitals—in return. Firms, households, and the state are therefore three channels through which money flows in one direction and goods and services flow in another. A fourth channel is the financial sector, which facilitates all kinds of financial transactions between the other three channels.

The two main flows are always interdependent, representing two different perspectives on the same economic exchange. They are circular because the money spent by households on goods and services is provided by the firms that both pay their wages and produce those goods and services.

## Encouraging efficiency

The circular flow is neither engineered nor designed and requires no direction from governments in order to function. So long as households, firms, and governments have access to a trusted medium of exchange—money, in particular—the flow arises naturally in a free market.

A free market is one in which the state upholds the rights of individuals and businesses to own private property and to control and transfer what they own as they see fit. It fosters the free flow of exchanges between buyers and sellers, and sellers compete with each other to provide buyers with goods and services that represent the best value for money. Competition not only helps keep prices low, it also encourages businesses to innovate and leads to specialization as some businesses become better at producing particular goods. In this way, businesses become more efficient and maximize their profits while both meeting the demands of consumers and employing workers with the relevant skills.

## An endless loop

Financial institutions, such as banks and brokerages, form the hub of a free-market economy (see pp.32–33). They offer loans and provide a forum in which bonds and other financial instruments can be traded. As such, they are key to the success of the circular flow between households, firms, and the state.

## LEAKAGES AND INJECTIONS

Any money from firms and households that is not spent directly in the exchange of domestic products is known as a "leakage" from the circular flow. This is because it does not contribute to economic activity. Paying taxes, buying imported products, and putting money into a savings account are examples of leakages. On the other hand, any money from international, state, or financial institutions that is spent directly in the exchange of domestic products is known as an "injection" into the circular flow. This is because it contributes to economic activity. Government spending, selling goods and services for export, and investing saved money are examples of injections. A circular flow is balanced when its leakages equal its injections.

### Households

Members of households exchange labor for wages to buy goods and services. They also pay taxes and receive the economic benefits of owning shares.

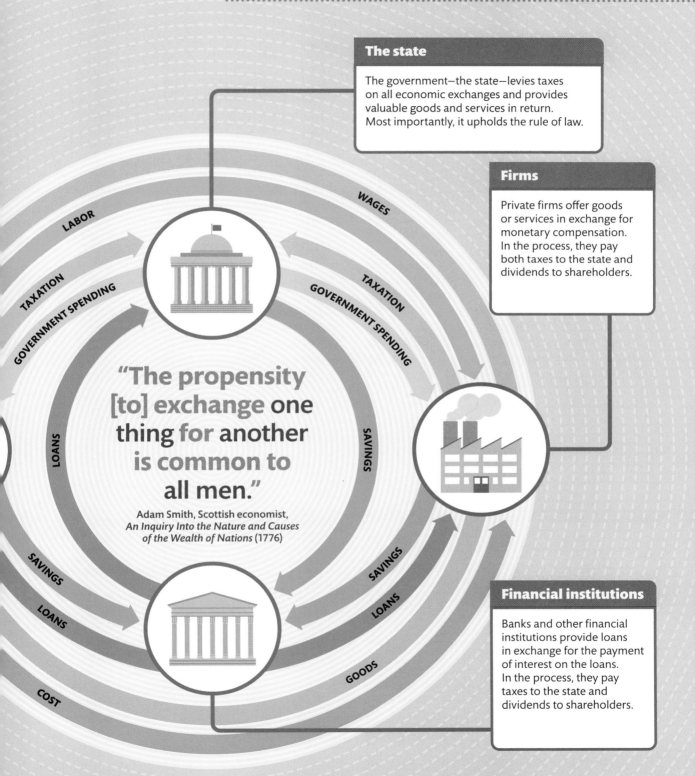

**The state**

The government—the state—levies taxes on all economic exchanges and provides valuable goods and services in return. Most importantly, it upholds the rule of law.

**Firms**

Private firms offer goods or services in exchange for monetary compensation. In the process, they pay both taxes to the state and dividends to shareholders.

**Financial institutions**

Banks and other financial institutions provide loans in exchange for the payment of interest on the loans. In the process, they pay taxes to the state and dividends to shareholders.

"The propensity [to] exchange one thing for another is common to all men."

Adam Smith, Scottish economist,
*An Inquiry Into the Nature and Causes of the Wealth of Nations* (1776)

LABOR

WAGES

TAXATION

TAXATION

GOVERNMENT SPENDING

GOVERNMENT SPENDING

LOANS

SAVINGS

SAVINGS

LOANS

SAVINGS

LOANS

COST

GOODS

# Economic indicators

The health of an economy, its predicted development, and how it might be improved are best understood by studying financial and human data ("indicators") and measuring their outcomes.

## Reading the signs

Economies pass through periods of ups and downs—between growth and recession (see pp.94–95)—known as economic cycles. Each cycle consists of four stages—expansion, peak, contraction, and trough—as an economy grows, reaches a high point, then slows down to reach a low point before rising again. A central feature of economics is the study of these fluctuating cycles, which last on average around five years and form part of a longer-term pattern of expansion and contraction.

To understand where an economy stands in its present cycle and how upward and downward trends might develop, economists study pieces of data, or indicators. This data is based on financial or market measurements, including inflation, wages, and commodity prices, and human factors, such as health, life expectancy, and education.

## Gathering the data

Most governments have statistical agencies that gather data from indicators so they can measure the state of the economic cycle. Economists analyze the data to explain the cycle, compare it to other periods, and predict its future behavior. Armed with this information, governments can draw up financial policies, businesses can decide on production targets, and investors can efficiently allocate capital. The publication of data can also have a noticeable impact on day-to-day household living, as it brings good or bad economic news that could affect areas such as taxation levels, wages, and price inflation.

# 17 months is the shortest-ever economic cycle in the US (1920–1921)

National Bureau of Economic Research (2023)

## Reading the indicators

An economy's ups and downs are measured across three types of indicators—leading, lagging, and coincident—each type relating to a particular point in the economic cycle. Leading indicators precede wider changes in the economy and are used in making predictions about the economy. Lagging indicators confirm changes that have already happened and are used to assess patterns in economic cycles. Coincident indicators reflect what is happening now, providing insight about the current state of an economy. Economists can study a wide range of indicators, although there are five key areas, or sectors, of activity (see right) common to all economies.

### Market rates

Leading indicators, reflecting fluctuations in prices—including those of commodities, such as oil, gas, metals, and wheat—as well as movements in foreign exchange rates and interest rates.

## Economic activity

Coincident indicators that measure the behavior of supply and demand in different economic sectors. These indicators are in turn influenced by market, labor, and inflation indicators.

## Balance of payments

Coincident indicators that follow the export and import flow of products and services, as well as international money transfers cleared by the banking system.

## Labor market

Lagging indicators, derived from business and household surveys, such as levels of employment and unemployment, number of job vacancies, and number of jobless benefit claims.

### Construction
The number of newly started building sites, how work on sites is progressing, and numbers of built units completed.

### Wages
Wage rises can be seen as a leading indicator for inflation. Increases in wage costs as firms strive to stay profitable are often passed on to consumers through higher prices.

## Inflation

Often viewed as a lagging indicator, inflation—the rate of price change of a fixed list of typical consumer items—is directly influenced by market rates and wages.

### Production
Combined industrial and manufacturing production, as well as raw materials and finished goods.

### Consumption
The total sales of goods and services to households.

## HUMAN DEVELOPMENT INDICATORS

The United Nations has created the Human Development Index (HDI) to highlight issues that affect a nation's progress beyond economic growth. The HDI offers four key indicators of well-being (see pp.144–145) based on three goals: a healthy life, a good education, and decent living standards.

### Health
❯ Life expectancy at birth

### Education
❯ Children's expected years at school
❯ Adults' average years of schooling

### Living standards
❯ Gross national income (GNI) per head of population

# Gross domestic product

**The most common measure of economic activity, gross domestic product (GDP) captures the value of transactions that happen in a country in a set period of time.**

## The size of an economy

GDP adds up the value of market-based transactions, so it does not include any personal production of goods and services. If you eat at a restaurant, your meal contributes to GDP, but if you prepare your meal with food you grew yourself, GDP does not change.

GDP measures activity within a certain time frame. If you sell a home built many years ago, GDP only takes into account the commissions and taxes paid during the transaction. However, if the home is newly built, GDP will reflect the value of the property itself.

As a measure of growth (see pp.90–91), GDP is a useful indicator of the health of an economy. Increasing GDP, or positive growth, contributes to higher employment, living standards, and spending power. Decreasing GDP, or negative growth, has the opposite effect and can even lead to recession (see pp.94–95).

## Nominal vs. real GDP

GDP can be measured in nominal terms or real terms. Nominal GDP gives the value of economic activity using the current price of goods and services. It is useful for comparing GDP against other economic factors, such as a nation's debt (see pp.112–113). Real GDP is the same measure but adjusted for inflation (see pp.96–97), so it removes the influence of any changes in prices from one period to the next. It allows for the fair comparison of economic activity across time periods or between countries.

### Household spending

The total spending by families on basic items such as food, clothing, housing, healthcare, entertainment, and transportation. This is often the largest component of GDP.

### Government spending

All government expenditure, including on public infrastructure, defense, education, healthcare, and interest payments on debt. Fiscal policy can be used to control business cycles (see pp.110–111).

## Demand-side GDP

One way to measure GDP is to add together the value of all the demand-side factors of the economy—that is, the total sales value of all the goods and services that are consumed within a country within a certain time period (see pp. 44–45). This demand can be divided into the four main drivers shown here.

# 70-80% of GDP in most countries comes from household and government spending

World Bank (2022)

## Investment spending

Firms' expenditure on capital goods such as equipment, buildings, and infrastructure. It also includes the value of goods held in inventories. This spending is driven by firms' expansion plans.

## Net exports

The value of a country's exports minus its imports. When exports exceed imports, it contributes positively to GDP. When imports exceed exports, it contributes negatively to GDP (see pp.176–177).

## SUPPLY-SIDE GDP

An alternative way to measure GDP, supply-side GDP is the total of all firms' "added value" (or "gross profits"). This is calculated as total revenues minus the costs incurred in producing the goods or services. Although supply-side GDP and demand-side GDP use data from different sources, their values are the same because "everything produced" equals "everything consumed."

## MEASURING PRODUCTIVITY

Comparisons of GDP across countries can be misleading. A rich country with a small population could have the same GDP as a poor country with a large population. To make comparisons more meaningful, economists look at productivity measures. "GDP per capita" is GDP divided by the population count. It captures how efficiently an economy is creating GDP.

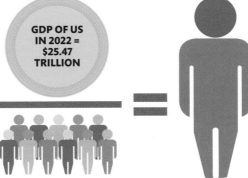

GDP OF US IN 2022 = $25.47 TRILLION

POPULATION OF US IN 2022 = 333 MILLION

GDP PER CAPITA OF US IN 2022 = $76,486

# Economic growth

Growth refers to changes in the amount of economic activity that occurs over time. Economies that grow at upward, steady rates tend to produce more prosperity and higher living standards.

## Positive and negative growth

Economists refer to the rate of economic growth as being positive (increasing) or negative (decreasing). Positive growth contributes to increased employment, improved living standards, and more opportunities for investing in public services such as healthcare and education. Negative growth equates to economic decline, which causes job losses and reduced spending power. Sustained negative growth leads to recession (see pp.94–95).

Economists separate economic growth into two distinct components: stable long-term positive growth and unstable short-term fluctuations.

## Drivers of growth

Long-term growth is affected by long-term supply and demand factors that are interconnected and often fuel each other. Supply depends on demographics, capital investment, and technological progress. Demand is determined by household consumption, business investment, international trade, and government expenditure. Countries with faster-growing economies tend to benefit from the positive effects of these supply and demand trends.

Some economists consider innovation and technological progress to be the fundamental driving force behind sustained economic growth. For them, human ingenuity and applied knowledge foster and enable positive trends in all the other supply and demand factors that drive economic activity.

**LONG-TERM SUPPLY TRENDS**

**Labor force**
The number of economically active people, as determined by the size of the population and the percentage of the population who are willing and able to work.

**Human capital**
The skills, knowledge, and experience of those engaged in economic production, achieved through both formal education and on-the-job training.

**Capital goods**
The number of active businesses, their financial resources, and some goods and infrastructure directly tied to economic production such as tools, machinery, and factories.

**Innovation**
The changes in operational efficiency of individual production units and how well they are integrated, as driven by specialization, mechanization, and scientific progress.

> # "Between 1900 and 2000, world GDP ... has increased about 19-fold ... an average annual rate of growth of 3%."
>
> International Monetary Fund, *Chapter V: The World Economy in the Twentieth Century* (2000)

## INCREASED ECONOMIC ACTIVITY

### LONG-TERM DEMAND TRENDS

**Household consumption**
The total household spending on goods and services as required to meet everyday needs for shelter, food, medical care, utilities, clothing, transportation, and entertainment.

**Investment**
The stock of durable goods and general-purpose infrastructure, such as buildings, homes, vehicles, roads, railways, and utility and telecommunications grids.

**Net exports**
The value of international trade as measured by the total value of exported goods and services subtracted from the total value of imports.

**Government consumption**
The total spending of the public sector, including government and public sector firms, since they consume goods and services from the private sector.

## BUSINESS CYCLES

The rate of economic growth is far from constant, and changes from one year to the next can be dramatic. Business cycles represent the short-term intervals of time that separate expansions (periods of positive growth) from contractions (periods of negative growth). The business cycle is often represented as a regular wave with peaks and troughs in between cycles of expansion and contraction. Despite periods of contraction, the overall rate of growth is usually positive in the long term.

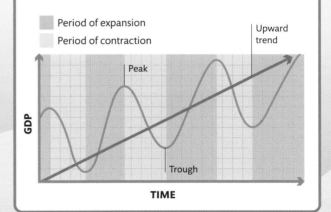

## A growing economy

Long-term economic growth can be understood by analyzing an economy's long-term supply and demand trends. However, it is worth noting that long-term trends can be disrupted by short-term fluctuations. Possible causes of this volatility are consumer confidence, shifts in government policy, or price changes.

# Savings and investments

**A country saves when it produces more than it consumes. These savings can finance investment, which may have a positive effect on the health of a national economy.**

## Potential growth

Investing (purchasing assets that can generate future income) and saving are often associated with personal finance, but the concepts apply at a national level, too. A country saves if it produces more goods and services than it needs; this excess is known as national savings. Excess production can be exported to countries that produce less than they consume. Or savings on goods and services can finance domestic investment, including spending on fixed assets—those intended for long-term use, such as technology, infrastructure, and building homes. These investments have the potential to bring lasting economic benefits.

Economists are interested in investment trends because they affect a country's ability to sustain high rates of economic expansion. Usually, countries with a high proportion of investment to GDP (the total value of a country's goods and services produced within a

specified period, usually a year— see pp.88–89) have high domestic savings rates, high rates of borrowing from other countries, and high rates of economic growth. A country's investment activities— along with other factors, such as the size of the workforce and the availability of natural resources— are related to its supply potential. This, in turn, has a direct bearing on GDP. In this way, investment decisions—by either the public (government funded) or private (business) sector—directly affect a country's potential GDP and long-term economic growth.

## Types of investment

This diagram explores different types of investments by the public or private sectors. Government fiscal (spending) policy finances investment via national savings (from any product that is not consumed) and by borrowing from other countries.

**Infrastructure**
Investment in infrastructure, which includes anything from highways and airports to telecommunication networks and energy plants. It typically unlocks a burst of economic growth.

**Durable goods**
The total expenditure on goods that generate benefits for their owners— everything from cars, planes, and home appliances to new production machines.

# 20–30% is the investment share of GDP in most countries in the world

The World Bank and Organization for Economic Co-operation and Development, national accounts data (1960–2022)

**Residential construction**
ll expenditure on buildings that are designed to serve as household residences. This investment adds to the stock of fixed assets in an economy.

**Software and intangibles**
The total amount that is spent on software and "intangible assets," such as trademarks, brand names, and copyright. These can add value over time—for example, through brand recognition.

**Total national investments**
All national savings and any money the country borrows from other countries (see box, below).

**Research and development**
All expenditure on investigative work that increases scientific and technological knowledge within firms. This can lead to indefinite economic benefits in the future.

**Inventories**
Any excess production becomes inventories that can be sold at a later stage. Inventories add to GDP when they are created, not when they are sold.

## THE FISCAL MULTIPLIER

Most government investment is spent on infrastructure and in research and development (R & D), since investment in these areas tends to unlock a disproportionately large amount of economic benefit over time. This phenomenon is known as a "positive fiscal multiplier," and it occurs when one currency unit (one dollar, for example) of public investment leads to more than one currency unit of GDP being created (see pp.88–89).

Government investment

Taxes/economic activity

## BORROWING AND LENDING

The total savings amount within a domestic economy is not always in balance with the amount a country invests each year (see pp.112–113). For example, when savings are insufficient to meet investment demands, a country can run a current-account deficit (borrowing from other countries), and when savings exceed investment demands, a country can run a current-account surplus (lending to other countries). These money flows across countries are called current-account imbalances.

# Recession

A recession is a prolonged period in which economic activity declines, causing unemployment, hardship for families and businesses, and a reduction in the country's GDP.

## What causes a recession?

Because populations increase—which creates jobs, spurs production, and stimulates innovation—the natural tendency for economies is to grow. However, usually after a prolonged period of growth, a major event—such as a war, a pandemic, or the collapse of a vital market (see pp.72–73)—can cause economic activity to slow or even stall for several months. When that happens, the economy is in recession.

Recessions are "shallow" when only a few industries are affected by the slow-down and "deep" when all sectors of the economy are affected simultaneously. Deep recessions can spread rapidly across the world, whereas shallow recessions may only affect domestic economies. Shallow recessions may even be triggered by policy; to reduce inflation (see pp.96–97), central banks often raise interest rates, which makes borrowing more expensive and reduces spending, which in turn reduces the upward pressure on prices.

## Dealing with recessions

Although recessions have many causes, they all have the same features: incomes decrease, asset prices fall, firms go out of business, and unemployment rises.

## Signs of a recession

Many economists define a recession as a period of economic decline that lasts for at least two three-month periods. The longest recession since World War II occurred in the US and lasted from the onset of the financial crisis of 2007–2008 (see pp.72–73) until June 2009. Recessions can be caused by unexpected disturbances to the economy, such as a sudden increase in prices, or by planned interventions, such as monetary policy.

## NEGATIVE CYCLE

When a recession begins, it starts a chain of events that increases and perpetuates the hardships felt across the economy. It causes firms to go bankrupt, which results in people losing their jobs and their incomes, which in turn causes households to consume less. These drops in spending cause other firms to go out of business, which leads to more unemployment, less spending, and so on. Many governments use fiscal and monetary policies to break this negative cycle.

UNEMPLOYMENT RISES

CONSUMERS SPEND LESS

SOLD

FIRMS SHUT DOWN

**Price increases**
Sudden increases in the price of commodities, such as fossil fuels, cause spikes in inflation rates, which suppress demand.

**Monetary policy**
Raising interest rates and raising taxes (see pp.114–115) decrease inflation but cause the economy to contract.

However, just as central banks can slow economies down, they can counteract recessions; by lowering interest rates, they encourage people to borrow and spend money, which in turn stimulates the economy. Although a recession may only last a few months, it can cause long-term damage, including deterring investment activity, which leads to a fall in GDP. It may also lead to structural unemployment, where old jobs are lost and not replaced, and unemployment persists beyond the recession.

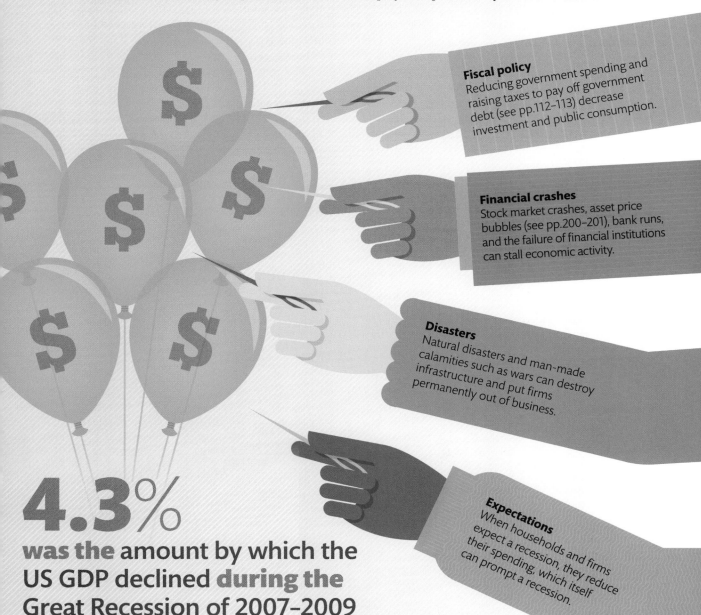

**Fiscal policy**
Reducing government spending and raising taxes to pay off government debt (see pp.112–113) decrease investment and public consumption.

**Financial crashes**
Stock market crashes, asset price bubbles (see pp.200–201), bank runs, and the failure of financial institutions can stall economic activity.

**Disasters**
Natural disasters and man-made calamities such as wars can destroy infrastructure and put firms permanently out of business.

**Expectations**
When households and firms expect a recession, they reduce their spending, which itself can prompt a recession.

# 4.3%
**was the amount by which the US GDP declined during the Great Recession of 2007–2009**
US Department of the Treasury (2013)

# Inflation

The increase in the price of goods and services over a given period of time is known as inflation. The inflation rate measures the rate of that increase, typically in relation to everyday household items.

## Consumer prices

Inflation is commonly understood as being the overall increase in the cost of living—in other words, the general increase in prices over a specific period of time, typically a year. However, inflation is in fact measured by studying the prices of specific sets of everyday goods and services, including food, alcohol, electricity, and even theater tickets. Government agencies decide which goods and services are included in this representational "basket" and update its contents as consumer preferences change over time. They also update the prices each month, collecting them from a sample of retailers and service providers. Finally, they record the prices in the consumer price index (CPI), which governments then use to gauge the inflation rate.

The CPI provides an estimate of the basket's overall price. To get the inflation rate, the CPI is divided by the price that the basket was a month or year earlier (depending on the period being analyzed), then multiplied by 100. For example, if

## Types of inflation

There are two main types of inflation: cost–push and demand–pull. Cost–push inflation is caused by supply, while demand–pull inflation is caused by demand. Economists call them "mechanical" causes, because they arise predictably from changes in "aggregate" (total) supply and demand.

### Cost-push inflation

Prices rise when the total supply for goods and services (aggregate supply) is less than consumer demand. This can occur when the price of raw materials rises.

**Price of raw materials**
The cost of production depends on the price of raw materials, such as oil.

**Cost of production increases**
If the price of raw materials rises, the cost of production rises, too.

**Production decreases**
Firms that are unable to operate at the higher price level decrease production but raise their prices to maintain their income.

**Contagion effect**
Higher costs spread to other sectors of the economy, which further increases prices.

the historic price was $140 and the current price is $150, then the CPI is 107, or inflation of 7 percent.

## A policy guide

The CPI is an invaluable tool for policymakers. It can indicate the extent to which wages must be adjusted in order for households to maintain their purchasing power (if inflation is at 7 percent, wages must rise by that same amount) and how much governments must increase welfare payments in order to protect people from poverty.

## ECONOMIC "SLACK"

"Slack" is a measure of the amount of unemployed resources in the economy, such as people out of work or machines standing idle. It is the difference between what the economy can produce and what it actually produces. When slack is high, inflation is low, because people are spending less. When slack is low, inflation rises, because people are spending more.

**POTENTIAL OUTPUT**

**ACTUAL OUTPUT**    **SLACK**

## Demand-pull inflation

Prices rise when the total demand for goods and services (aggregate demand) exceeds supply. This can happen during economic booms, when consumer confidence is high.

**Increased consumer demand**
Demand increases due to consumer confidence, government investment, or low inflation.

SOLD OUT

**Demand outstrips supply**
When demand outstrips supply, prices rise. This is because people are willing to pay extra for the product.

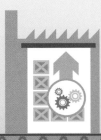

**Production increases**
Firms tend to increase production when demand is high.

**Firms hire more workers**
Higher production increases the demand for labor. This raises wages (a form of inflation) as competition for workers increases.

## "Double-digit inflation is a terrible thing."
Paul Volcker, chairman of the US Federal Reserve (1979–1987)

# Unemployment and labor

**The unemployment rate—the share of people without a job but looking for one—is closely tied to economic activity. Changes in the labor market directly affect governments, firms, and consumers.**

### Labor highs and lows

Governments and market experts closely monitor the unemployment level in a population for insights into the present and future health of an economy. Unemployment is classified by economists as a lagging indicator—an ongoing measurable feature that can help predict economic trends (see pp.86–87).

In general terms, when economic activity—the creation, selling, and buying of goods and services—is high, there is an increased demand for labor, and unemployment falls. When activity is low, firms reduce their workforce, and unemployment rises. These labor changes happen slowly, however, and it is only after a sustained period of economic growth or decline that the rates of unemployment alter significantly. During economic expansion, firms try to meet the increased demand for products and services by increasing productivity before hiring more workers. In downturns, firms first reduce working hours before they fire staff.

## Work and the population

The working-age population of a nation is defined as all individuals above a minimum age (usually 16, but less in some countries) and below the official age of retirement. Most of those—the labor force—will either be working at a job or out of work looking for a job.

### In and out of labor

Members of the working-age population who are unable to work are not included in the labor force or in unemployment rate calculations.

**WORKING-AGE POPULATION**

**LABOR FORCE**

**Employed**
Those who are currently in a paid job either part-time or full-time.

**Unemployed**
Those who do not currently have a job but are actively looking for a job.

**Outside labor force**
Those who are neither employed nor looking for a job, also known as inactive population.

## Pressures on numbers

Frictions within the labor market can cause unemployment. For example, job seekers who refuse to work for a wage lower than their reservation wage—the minimum they would accept for a particular job—remain unemployed for longer. Also, some firms may fail to hire more workers because they cannot find individuals with the required skills or because such workers are not based in the same geographical area as the hiring firms.

## LABOR MARKETS

Labor is subject to the same basic economic concepts of supply and demand as goods and services (see pp.44–45). Workers supply labor in exchange for money (wages), while firms demand labor and pay wages. Higher wages reduce the demand for labour (the downward demand curve) but increase the supply of labour (the upward supply curve).

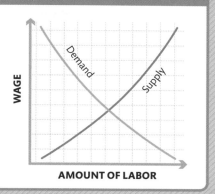

WAGE

Demand

Supply

**AMOUNT OF LABOR**

# "Labor was the first price, the original purchase-money."

Adam Smith, Scottish economist and philosopher, *The Wealth of Nations* (1776)

## Types of unemployment

Different factors influence the circumstances under which individuals are unemployed. These are all components of the unemployment rate.

WORK

NO WORK

### Cyclical unemployment
Follows the economic cycle. High unemployment is often associated with downturns in the economy.

### Frictional unemployment
The creation and finding of jobs may face obstacles. Such "frictions" in the labor market can add to unemployment.

### Structural unemployment
Change in the structure of an economy, such as the development of job automation, can create unemployment.

## UNEMPLOYMENT RATE

A country's unemployment rate is calculated by taking the number of people currently unemployed and actively looking for a job, dividing it by the total labor force (employed and unemployed individuals), then multiplying by 100 to produce a percentage. The rate is generally based on those actively seeking work in the past four weeks and free to start work in the next two weeks.

UNEMPLOYMENT RATE

| 2 MILLION UNEMPLOYED PEOPLE |
|---|
| 40 MILLION LABOR FORCE |

x 100 = **5%**

# The Phillips curve

A graph known as the Phillips curve depicts the relationship between inflation and economic activity. It is commonly used by policymakers and market participants to predict inflation given prevailing economic conditions.

## Interpreting the curve

The Phillips curve illustrates the idea that there is an inverse relationship between unemployment and inflation (see pp.96–97)—in other words, that when unemployment is high, inflation is low, and vice versa. It is named after New Zealand economist William Phillips (1914–1975), who discovered and studied this relationship. Today, economists tend to interpret the curve more broadly as depicting the relationship between inflation and measures of economic activity.

For example, when economic activity is high, demand is high, firms produce more, and more workers are employed, which leads to more spending, higher prices (inflation), and lower unemployment.

Under current versions of the Phillips curve, inflation is often related to the concept of the "output gap"— that is, the difference between what an economy is producing and what it can produce. If the output gap is positive, then the economy is overworking to meet a high demand, which leads to inflation.

## Inflation and unemployment

The inverse relationship between inflation and unemployment is depicted in the classic Phillips curve (shown in the first graph here). However, in the 1970s, there was a period in which countries across the world experienced both high unemployment and high inflation simultaneously (shown in the second graph). This was caused by a rise in the price of oil. More recently, further rises in the price of oil and the cost of COVID-19 lockdown measures have had similar effects.

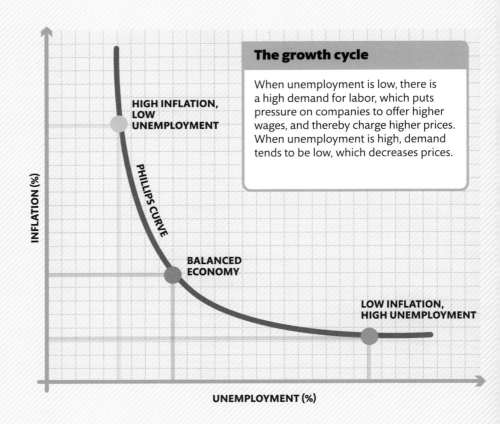

HIGH INFLATION, LOW UNEMPLOYMENT

PHILLIPS CURVE

BALANCED ECONOMY

LOW INFLATION, HIGH UNEMPLOYMENT

INFLATION (%)

UNEMPLOYMENT (%)

### The growth cycle

When unemployment is low, there is a high demand for labor, which puts pressure on companies to offer higher wages, and thereby charge higher prices. When unemployment is high, demand tends to be low, which decreases prices.

## A flattening of the curve?

The effects of inflation and economic activity on each other have become weaker in recent decades, suggesting that the Phillips curve has flattened. This phenomenon has prompted debates among academics and politicians on the relevance of the Phillips curve today. However, it remains crucial for monetary policymakers (see pp.114–115). If a policymaker believes that the curve is steep, then they may decide to raise interest rates—which encourages people to save—during times of low unemployment to bring inflation down. On the other hand, if they believe that the curve is flat—in other words, that economic activity has only a small effect on inflation—then they may resist raising interest rates.

### THE ROLE OF EXPECTATIONS

An interesting element in the relationship between unemployment and inflation—the two variables of the Phillips curve—is the role played by expectations (see pp.106-107). For example, firms set their prices on what they expect inflation will be in the future: if they think it will be higher, then they are likely to increase their prices to prepare for it. Likewise, workers tend to ask for higher wages to maintain their purchasing power if they expect inflation to be higher in the future. In other words, the mere expectation of higher inflation can lead to higher inflation—which economists in turn have to allow for when making economic predictions.

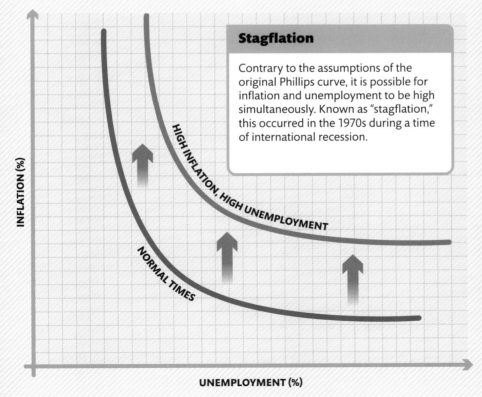

### Stagflation

Contrary to the assumptions of the original Phillips curve, it is possible for inflation and unemployment to be high simultaneously. Known as "stagflation," this occurred in the 1970s during a time of international recession.

HIGH INFLATION, HIGH UNEMPLOYMENT

NORMAL TIMES

INFLATION (%)

UNEMPLOYMENT (%)

"The Phillips curve ... moved with remarkable speed from the economics journals to the policy process."

Allan Meltzer, American economist, *A History of the Federal Reserve* (2003)

# Aggregate supply and aggregate demand

Economists use aggregate supply and demand to measure all goods and services produced or consumed in an economy. These measures allow economists to follow the wider economic effects of price changes.

## Aggregating the market

In economics, "aggregate" means "total." While rules of supply and demand (see pp.44–45) apply to specific goods or services, aggregate supply (AS) and aggregate demand (AD) apply to all goods and services. Similarly, AS and AD are linked not to specific prices but to the value of all prices—the "aggregate price level." By looking at the interactions between supply and demand for all markets, economists can judge how to deal with issues that affect the whole economy, such as inflation and unemployment (see pp.96–99).

## A wider price picture

Like individual demand for goods and services, AD usually falls as prices rise and vice versa, but due to three wider economic factors. First, in what is known

## The aggregate economy

At the macroeconomic level, aggregate supply and aggregate demand cover all markets for goods and services within the whole economy. Their movements are dictated by the aggregate price level.

### AGGREGATE SUPPLY

The total supply of goods and services is limited by the economy's capacity to maximize its production factors, which fall into four main groups: workforce, technology, physical capital, and human capital.

### AS VS. PRICE

When aggregate prices are low, firms scale down production because profit margins are lower. When prices rise, margins also rise, so firms produce more. However, output is ultimately limited by the available level of production factors.

WORKFORCE   TECHNOLOGY   PHYSICAL CAPITAL   HUMAN CAPITAL

as the "wealth effect," a rise or fall in the aggregate price reduces or increases the value of people's assets, dampening or boosting consumer demand. Second, if monetary policy (see pp.114–115) raises tax or interest rates, the aggregate price rises and AD falls—but then rises if rates are cut. Third, if an economy's prices rise relative to those in other economies, exports of its goods and services reduce (see pp.156–157) and AD falls. More competitive prices raise exports and AD.

When aggregate prices are low, so is AS, as lower profit margins reduce production. When aggregate prices are high, so are profits, leading to greater output. However, this increasing output will hit a limit, which is determined by availability of capital, labor, and the quality of technology. Attempts to push production beyond this point only lead to higher prices.

# "... demand and supply are matters of mathematics, not guesswork."

Elbert Hubbard, American philosopher,
*The Philosophy of Elbert Hubbard* (1916)

## AD-AS MODEL

When graphed, the AS and AD curves depict the relationship between prices and output across the economy. Higher prices reduce demand but induce supply. Eventually, however, supply hits a constraint and there is no capacity to produce more at any price. At this point AS is vertical.

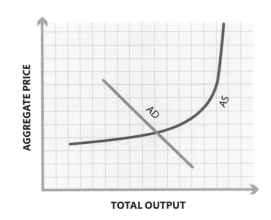

## AGGREGATE DEMAND

AD is the combined value of all goods and services, capital goods (total property and equipment of all firms), net exports (exports minus imports), and government spending.

## AD VS. PRICE

The more aggregate prices rise, the more AD falls. AD is limited only by aggregate prices—if they are low enough, then demand, unlike supply, is potentially unlimited.

GOODS & SERVICES

CAPITAL GOODS

NET EXPORTS

GOVERNMENT SPENDING

# ⬛ Market equilibrium

**A balance in supply and demand ensures stable prices across markets. When this is not the case, adjusting prices helps reset quantities of goods and services and return economic equilibrium.**

## Demand does not always equal supply

When the quantities of goods and services supplied and demanded are in balance, there are no surpluses or shortages. As a result, there are no price fluctuations in the markets, and inflation—the normal rate at which prices rise (see pp.96–97)—remains stable.

When there is a change in either the demand or supply (see pp.44–45) of goods and services, known as demand or supply "shocks," efficient markets tend to adjust their prices accordingly to help quantities rebalance and equilibrium return. After such price adjustments, the new differences in quantities and prices show that the economy has returned to a new state of equilibrium.

## Dealing with market shocks

An example of a demand shock is when a government substantially increases its spending on infrastructure, which in turn increases the demand for construction materials and engineering services. The supply for these goods and services is unlikely to change immediately, which means that, for the time being,

## Balancing supply and demand

Aggregate supply (AS) and aggregate demand (AD) are the total supply and demand in an economy at a given time (see pp.102–103). These diagrams show how economies can move from one equilibrium to another with changes in AS. Prices adjust to create a new equilibrium.

# 2%

**is the expected rate of inflation in developed countries when aggregate supply and aggregate demand are balanced**

US Federal Reserve inflation guidance

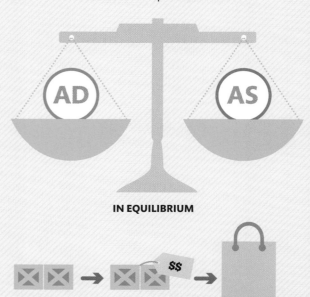

**Market equilibrium**
When quantities supplied (inventories) and demanded are equal, there is no reason for prices to change and an economy is in a state of equilibrium.

**AD** **AS**

**IN EQUILIBRIUM**

**STABLE INVENTORY** → **STABLE PRICE** $$ → **STABLE CONSUMER SPENDING**

there is more demand than supply, which causes an expected increase in prices. These price increases are a market mechanism that returns the economy to equilibrium—in this example, they may dissuade some from carrying out private construction jobs, which are now more expensive to complete. The resulting reduction in demand helps rebalance supply and demand. However, this new equilibrium has higher prices and higher quantities—a typical dynamic with demand shocks.

Conversely, an adverse supply shock usually creates a new equilibrium where there are higher prices but lower quantities. For instance, where a very bad winter decreases crop production substantially, this reduces supply. Market adjustments increase prices as a way of restricting demand, given the smaller supply.

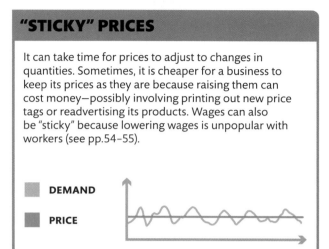

## "STICKY" PRICES

It can take time for prices to adjust to changes in quantities. Sometimes, it is cheaper for a business to keep its prices as they are because raising them can cost money—possibly involving printing out new price tags or readvertising its products. Wages can also be "sticky" because lowering wages is unpopular with workers (see pp.54–55).

DEMAND

PRICE

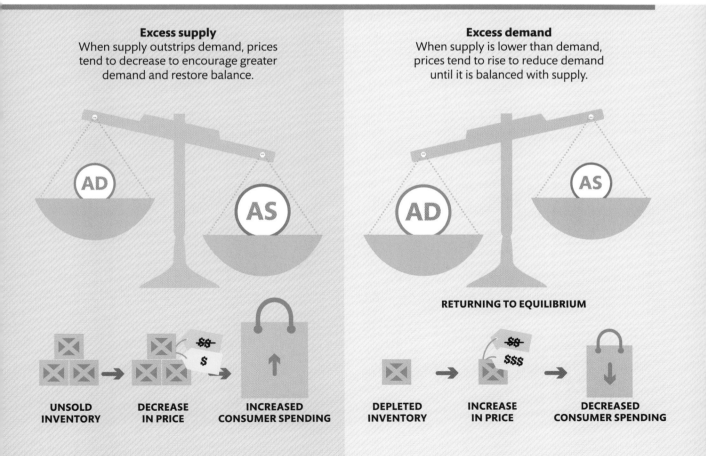

**Excess supply**
When supply outstrips demand, prices tend to decrease to encourage greater demand and restore balance.

**Excess demand**
When supply is lower than demand, prices tend to rise to reduce demand until it is balanced with supply.

**RETURNING TO EQUILIBRIUM**

UNSOLD INVENTORY → DECREASE IN PRICE → INCREASED CONSUMER SPENDING

DEPLETED INVENTORY → INCREASE IN PRICE → DECREASED CONSUMER SPENDING

# Expectations

**Beliefs, or expectations, about what will happen to price inflation in the future affect how products and services perform today. Understanding those expectations can help control prices and stabilize the economy.**

## Securing the future

Expectations about inflation (see pp.96–97) reflect what consumers, firms, and investors think will happen to prices of products and services in the future. Decisions based on those expectations can also affect what happens to prices today. If the expectation is that prices are likely to increase over the next year, firms will tend to adjust what they charge for their products or services to protect their profits, while workers may ask for wage increases to maintain their purchasing power. Expectations around price increases can also influence how individuals invest, borrow, and spend. To keep prices stable and avoid excessive fluctuations in the fortunes of firms and markets (see pp.104–105), it is crucial to control inflation expectations.

## "Unanchored" or "anchored"

When expectations are based largely on short-term price changes, they are said to be "unanchored." For example, if oil prices increase suddenly, some

## Looking backward and forward

To understand inflation expectations, economists consider how different individuals form their beliefs about how prices might change. People tend to either look backward, basing their expectations on what has happened to inflation in the past, or forward, to what might happen given present financial circumstances. Some combine both methods to update their expectations.

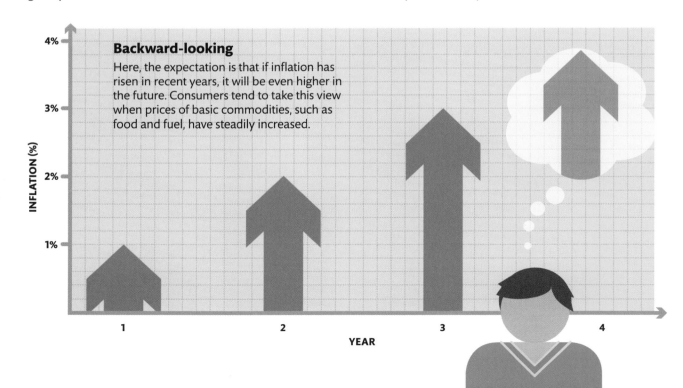

### Backward-looking

Here, the expectation is that if inflation has risen in recent years, it will be even higher in the future. Consumers tend to take this view when prices of basic commodities, such as food and fuel, have steadily increased.

INFLATION (%)

4%
3%
2%
1%

1    2    3    4

YEAR

individuals might believe that inflation rates over the next year will be higher as a result. Conversely, when expectations are not a reaction to current prices, they are "anchored." In this situation, individuals base their expectations not on price shocks in the present, but on the belief that prices in the future will remain stable.

Central banks, which manage money on a national level, try to keep inflation expectations anchored so that sudden price changes do not destabilize prices in the future. They do so mainly through public policy announcements—for example, explaining how they would react to future price developments and giving clear targets for inflation rates. If the bank is credible, individuals are likely to believe that inflation will match the target, and expectations will be anchored.

## MEASURING EXPECTATIONS

> **Public surveys** A sample of firms and consumers is asked—on a regular basis—how much they expect prices to change, usually up to 10 years ahead.

> **Inflation forecasts** Economists and other financial experts publish their opinions on future price rises.

> **Market-based inflation expectations** These are measured by finding the difference in profits—money earned—over time between two financial instruments (see pp.188–189), such as bonds or loans, where one is adjusted for inflation and the other is not.

# "The economy generally does not waste information."

John Muth, American economist and creator of the rational expectations theory (1961)

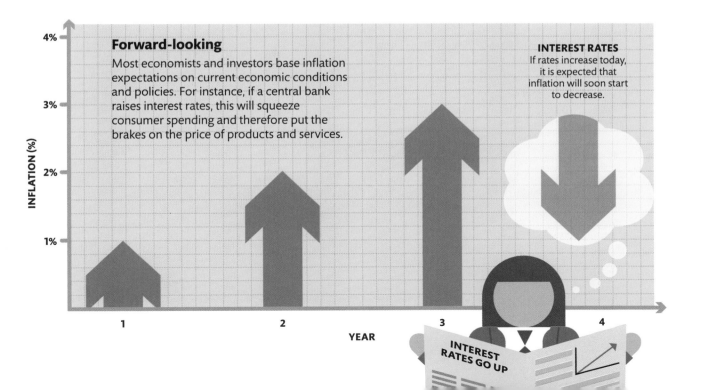

**Forward-looking**

Most economists and investors base inflation expectations on current economic conditions and policies. For instance, if a central bank raises interest rates, this will squeeze consumer spending and therefore put the brakes on the price of products and services.

**INTEREST RATES**
If rates increase today, it is expected that inflation will soon start to decrease.

INFLATION (%)

4%

3%

2%

1%

1        2        3        4

YEAR

INTEREST RATES GO UP

# The role of government

From an economic perspective, governments are essential for organizing large-scale projects that involve the coordination of vast economic resources and benefit large swathes of society.

## The common interest

Economics is a social science that is devoted to understanding the use and distribution of scarce resources by competing individuals or groups (see pp.14–15). However, people do not simply compete—they also coordinate to divide resources, and for this, centralized governments are needed.

The nature and extent of government power is determined by each country's political system. Governments typically raise money via taxation and deliver goods and services that meet preestablished common interests. Economically, government action is efficient when it is guided by clear objectives and prevents conflicts of interest that might otherwise arise between competing people or groups. It can also reap the benefits of economies of scale, whereby products become cheaper when they are bought in large quantities (see pp.50–51). Areas such as education and healthcare benefit directly from this. For example, governments can negotiate discounts when buying large amounts of medicine or books and equipment for schools and colleges.

## State action

There are six key ways in which governments can influence economies. Although few countries have exactly the same priorities, all have to reconcile their need for state action with the need for taxes to pay for it.

### Economic agent

The state buys goods and services from private firms and manages state-owned enterprises. Its policies can also influence the economy (see pp.110–111).

### Regulator

The government sets regulations to hinder unscrupulous market behavior, defend consumers' interests, and protect the environment.

### Provider of incentives

Government subsidies and targeted taxation affect the market by encouraging or penalizing particular economic activities.

**TAXES**

## Provider of public services

Governments provide basic social services, such as education, healthcare, emergency services, trash collection, security, and social care.

## Preserver of law and order

The state provides an accessible and impartial justice system in which contracts can be upheld and enforced and human rights are protected.

## Provider of social welfare

A government-controlled welfare system provides social housing, state pensions, unemployment benefits, and disability assistance.

## Government intervention

Any economic interaction can potentially lead to conflicts of interest, so it may benefit from government intervention. The state takes control of legislation, the judiciary, public security, and national defense because these areas are too important to be entrusted to private companies. Other ways that governments can influence the economy include regulating the market, participating in it via state-controlled enterprises, and controlling the money supply through fiscal policies such as taxation (see pp.110–111).

## POLITICAL PHILOSOPHIES

A government's role is influenced by its political beliefs. Laws considered useful by one country and for the "common good" might be regarded as interference by another. Each society decides how to balance the role of the state with individual freedoms. In 1969, American activist David Nolan (1943–2010) created the Nolan Chart. It shows a continuum of five views, based on how much the state should intervene in personal and economic issues.

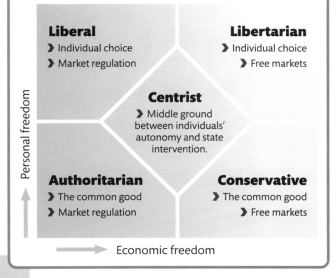

**Liberal**
> Individual choice
> Market regulation

**Libertarian**
> Individual choice
> Free markets

**Centrist**
> Middle ground between individuals' autonomy and state intervention.

**Authoritarian**
> The common good
> Market regulation

**Conservative**
> The common good
> Free markets

Personal freedom

Economic freedom

**SPENDING**

# ⅈ Fiscal policy

A government's fiscal policy is the way it taxes and spends in order to stabilize the economy. The form of this policy depends on many factors, including whether the economy is expanding or contracting.

## Objectives

A government can influence GDP (see pp.88–89) either directly, by changing its spending, or indirectly, by changing its tax policies. The goals of fiscal policy can be short term (aimed at counteracting the business cycle and stabilizing economic activity, see p.91) or long term (focused on economic growth or reducing poverty). These goals are usually reached by spending on infrastructure, innovation, education, health, and pension reforms. In contrast to monetary policy (see pp.114–115), fiscal policy can target specific firms, households, or economic sectors. For example, the government may make regular income payments to poorer households, which both reduces poverty and raises the overall income level of the population. Two important fiscal policy tools are automatic stabilizers and fiscal stimulus. Automatic stabilizers are tax and spending changes that are built into the system but do not depend on direct actions by the government. For example, during a downturn, the amount of taxes collected decreases as firms' profits

## With or against the cycle?

Fiscal policy can be applied in a stabilizing manner by stimulating production and consumption in downturns and restricting it during booms. However, it can also magnify the cycle's fluctuations, which can have disastrous consequences.

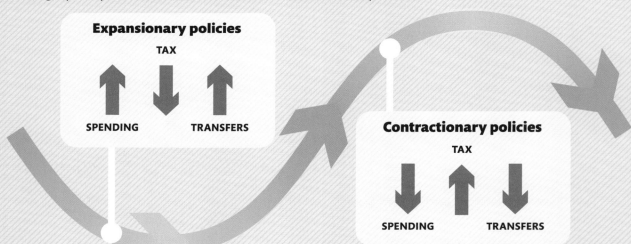

**Expansionary policies**

TAX

SPENDING    TRANSFERS

**Contractionary policies**

TAX

SPENDING    TRANSFERS

### Countercyclical policy

The government increases spending and transfers (payments made to individuals through social programs such as welfare) and cuts taxes to stimulate growth when the economy is contracting. Likewise, it cuts spending and raises taxes when the economy is expanding—a measure that helps curb inflation (see pp.90–91).

and households' income decrease, but social benefits increase. Fiscal stimulus, on the other hand, refers to the government's ability to spend money (for example, on public work programs) or cut taxes in order to stimulate economic activity. Such measures can target specific groups, but they can take time to have effect.

The effectiveness of the fiscal stimulus is called the fiscal multiplier, which measures the effect of a $1 change in spending or a $1 change in tax revenue on the level of GDP (see p.93).

## DIRECT AND INDIRECT TAXATION

Direct taxes are paid directly to the government by individuals or firms. Examples of these are income tax, corporate tax, inheritance tax, and capital gains tax. Indirect taxes are charged by the government to intermediaries, such as producers and retailers, who pass the charge on to the consumer. Examples of these are value added tax (VAT), customs duty, and landfill taxes.

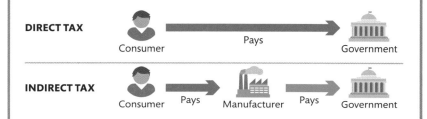

**DIRECT TAX** — Consumer — Pays → Government

**INDIRECT TAX** — Consumer — Pays → Manufacturer — Pays → Government

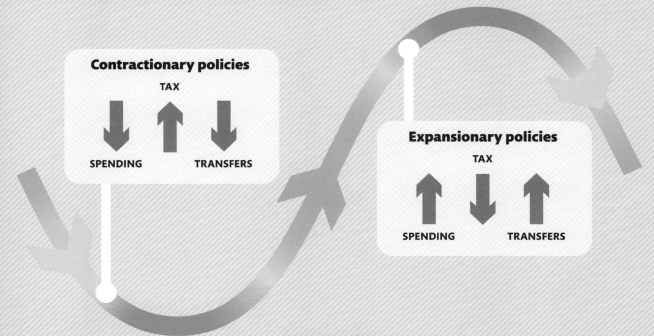

### Contractionary policies
**TAX**
SPENDING     TRANSFERS

### Expansionary policies
**TAX**
SPENDING     TRANSFERS

## Procyclical policy

The government cuts spending and raises taxes when the economy is contracting and increases spending and cuts taxes when the economy is expanding. Such measures may be necessary in emergencies, but they are usually pursued when governments are ill advised or are unable to borrow money.

# Government borrowing

Governments borrow money when their planned expenditures exceed what they can raise through taxation. To provide the money, lenders buy government investments called "securities."

## Balancing the books

All governments are responsible for financing public services, such as health and education, and they pay for this largely through taxation. Like householders, governments set budgets—"fiscal plans"—for different areas of expenditure based on estimates for expected outgoings and income. Sometimes, tax income creates a budget surplus, but governments often cannot raise enough money to pay for services and have to borrow to cover deficits—periods of debt. How much a government borrows depends partly on changing seasonal factors, such as the weather, public holidays, and spikes in consumer spending. It will also take into account any potential income surpluses, such as the taxation of excess profits in the energy industries.

## Dealing with deficits

Once a government has allocated budgets for a country's public services and taken into account its tax and other revenues, there is likely to be a shortfall in funds—a budget deficit. The government then has two options: print more money or (more realistically) borrow. Most governments are able to manage their levels of debt. If not, they have to seek help from an international lender.

### Borrowing

Governments borrow money by selling securities to investors in financial markets. These are effectively short- and long-term loans.

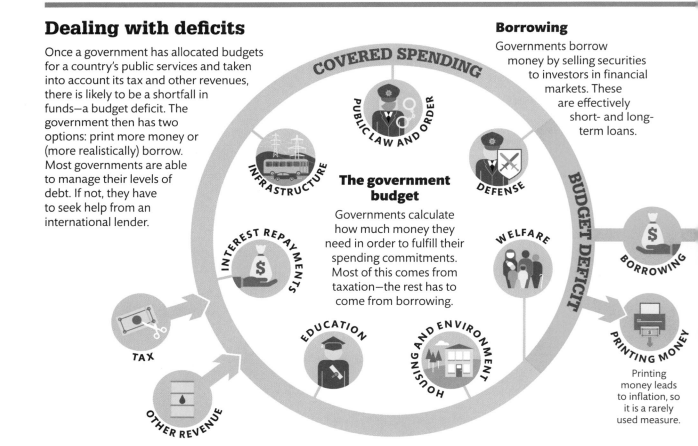

**COVERED SPENDING**

PUBLIC LAW AND ORDER

INFRASTRUCTURE

DEFENSE

INTEREST REPAYMENTS

WELFARE

**The government budget**

Governments calculate how much money they need in order to fulfill their spending commitments. Most of this comes from taxation—the rest has to come from borrowing.

BUDGET DEFICIT

BORROWING

EDUCATION

HOUSING AND ENVIRONMENT

TAX

OTHER REVENUE

PRINTING MONEY

Printing money leads to inflation, so it is a rarely used measure.

## Buying and selling debt

Instead of borrowing money from a bank, governments sell "securities." These are bonds—loans made by investors with the guarantee of full repayment at a set future time and with periodic interest bonuses, or "coupons" (see pp.204–205). Such bonds are a low-risk investment and popular in domestic markets. If there is a stable balance between the overall national debt and the GDP—the total value of the products and services a country generates (see pp.88–89)—a government is in a good position to expand its debt and will likely find ample funding. However, if a government faces a sudden crisis, such as a war or a pandemic, it may have to borrow money that pushes the economy into deficit. In this situation, local financial markets will be less willing to buy bonds, and the government may be forced to borrow in foreign markets, where fluctuations in currency exchange rates may expose it to costlier debt repayments. A government that struggles to sell securities may have to turn to an international lender, such as the IMF (see right).

### THE IMF

The International Monetary Fund (IMF) is a financial agency of the United Nations. It lends money to governments with unsustainable debts, allowing them to avoid financial collapse at a national level. In return, the IMF expects governments to take economic actions—agreed on with the IMF—that will bring their debt under control. A government will approach the IMF only when all other borrowing options have failed.

### Local-currency securities

Governments issue securities in the form of bonds in their own—local—currency, which protects them from financial shocks that might happen in foreign markets.

#### BONDS

These are loans made by investors to a government. The repayment date for a bond—when it "matures"—can be as short as one month in the future, although governments usually issue longer-term bonds of up to 30 years (sometimes longer) to finance their budget deficits.

### Foreign-currency securities

Governments can also issue securities in different currencies in foreign financial markets, where they are subject to volatility in currency exchange rates.

### Government default

If governments "default" on their debts—fail to pay them—they will be unable to borrow the money they need for a country to operate. At this point, they usually apply to the IMF (see above) for help.

# Monetary policy

**Monetary policy is set by a central bank to promote price stability. The bank takes steps to fuel or dampen economic activity in a bid to keep inflation within a target range while encouraging long-term growth.**

## The role of central banks

A country's central bank normally sets monetary policy, whereas government usually controls fiscal policy (see pp.110–111). Both forms of intervention are designed to influence how the economy is performing. The goal is to create price stability so people can plan how much to spend, save, and invest, which in turn fosters employment and economic growth (see pp.90–91).

In their pursuit for price stability, many central banks across the developed world currently aim for an inflation rate of 2 percent per year. In some cases, central banks have a "dual mandate," meaning that they simultaneously try to maximize employment.

Decisions on monetary policy are taken at policy-making meetings, usually followed by a press conference in which the central bank explains the reasons behind its decision and makes forecasts for the economy and for interest rates.

## Influencing the economy

Broadly speaking, monetary policy attempts to indirectly stimulate either spending or saving, but it cannot directly control these.

When there is too much demand relative to the capacity of the economy, inflation tends to rise and unemployment declines. In this case, the central bank tries to stabilize the economy by restricting demand through a tightening of its monetary policy, which increases interest rates. This is called a "contractionary policy." Conversely, when demand is slow, inflation declines and unemployment rises. Demand can be fueled through the central bank relaxing its monetary policy and decreasing interest rates, which is an "expansionary policy."

## HELICOPTER MONEY

Named after the helicopters that drop emergency supplies, "helicopter money" is an extreme policy for stimulating the economy. It passes money from the central bank directly to the public, for example, through relief payments to firms. In 2020, during the COVID-19 pandemic, households and firms in the US received direct payments designed to stimulate spending. Helicopter money can be paid as a form of monetary policy enacted by the central bank or as a type of fiscal policy undertaken by government. Helicopter money is different from quantitative easing (see opposite) because it transfers money to people directly instead of indirectly through changes in interest rates.

# 0–2%

**was the early 1990s inflation goal for New Zealand—the first country to set a formal target**

David Archer, New Zealand economist,
*Inflation Targeting in New Zealand* (2000)

# Tools of a central bank

Central banks have numerous tools at their disposal for controlling interest rates and therefore the cost of capital. This allows them to indirectly influence the amount of money in circulation. The cheaper it is to borrow money, the more people will spend, which stimulates the economy. Whereas, when borrowing gets more expensive, people borrow and spend less. After the 2007–2008 financial crash (see pp.72–73), new unconventional tools were also used.

## Conventional tools

### Setting interest rates
The central bank sets the interest rate it charges banks for borrowing or pays them for lending money. This affects rates across the market. Lower rates mean cheaper borrowing; higher rates make borrowing less attractive.

### Setting reserve requirements
Commercial banks must legally hold a percentage of their deposits as cash. Changing the required level of these reserves increases or reduces how much banks can lend and therefore how much money is in circulation.

### Open market operations
An open market operation is when the central bank buys or sells securities (see pp.188–189) on the open market. This influences the interest rates banks use to lend to each other and so how much money is available.

### Discount window
The discount window is a service where the central bank makes very short-term loans to banks. Changing how much it lends has the effect of increasing or reducing the flow of credit to households and businesses.

## Unconventional tools

### Quantitative easing
By buying government debt in the form of bonds (see pp.204–205), the central bank can lower interest rates—mostly in the long term—and inject money into circulation.

### Quantitative tightening
The reverse of quantitative easing, the central bank can sell government bonds to increase interest rates and reduce the amount of money in circulation.

**STIMULATING THE ECONOMY**

**DAMPENING THE ECONOMY**

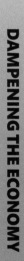

# The role of banks

In modern economies, the money supply is controlled by commercial banks, which operate under the guidance of the monetary policy set by the country's central bank.

## Types of money

Money exists in two distinct forms. On the one hand, there is a nation's "currency," which is issued by the central bank (the country's commercial bank regulator) and exists as coins and paper bills. On the other hand, there is electronic money, which exists as bank deposits held by commercial banks on behalf of depositors. As most of the money in circulation is electronic, commercial banks therefore play a crucial role in the creation of money—which they do by issuing loans to borrowers.

## Controlling money

A commercial bank creates a new deposit when it extends a new loan to a borrower. It does this by lending money from savings that belong to other depositors—a practice that only works because it is unlikely that all of the bank's customers will spend their money at once. However, there is a minimum amount of money that banks are required to keep in reserve so that customers can always make withdrawals. This amount, which is a percentage of the bank's total holdings, is determined by the central bank and varies depending on the state of the economy. If inflation is high (see pp.96–97), the reserve level may be increased to reduce the amount of money banks can lend.

## How banks create money

Banks create money by extending more loans than they hold in deposits. The amount they create is limited by demand and by regulations concerning how much money they must hold in reserve and what interest rates they should charge. However, when a bank lends money, the borrower often spends it on goods or services provided by other customers of the bank, who then redeposit the money, which the bank lends again.

**First deposit**
A customer deposits $1,000 into a bank account. If the reserve rate is 10 percent, the bank keeps $100 in reserve and lends the remaining $900.

**$1,000 DEPOSIT**

**$900 DEPOSIT $100 RESERVE**

**$900 LOAN**

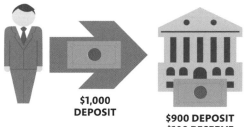

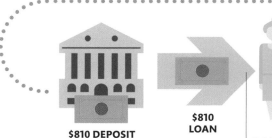

**$810 DEPOSIT $90 RESERVE**

**$810 LOAN**

**$810 TRANSACTION**

At this point, there is $2,810 in circulation.

**Second and third deposits**
A second customer borrows $900 and spends it on goods provided by a third customer, who returns the money to the bank—which keeps $90 in reserve and lends the remaining $810.

During a recession, it may be reduced to release more money into the economy (see pp.114–115).

When the central bank's policy is to reduce inflation, it sets a base rate (a benchmark interest rate), and commecial banks respond by raising their lending rates. This reduces demand for lending and increases saving. When there is a deflation risk, the central bank will lower the base rate, which leads to increased lending, and therefore more economic activity.

## HOW DO BANKS WORK?

Banks work by collecting deposits from savers and extending loans to borrowers. Their profitability depends on collecting more interest from borrowers than paying interest to savers.

At this point, there is $1,900 in circulation from the first customer's $1,000 deposit and the bank's $900 loan.

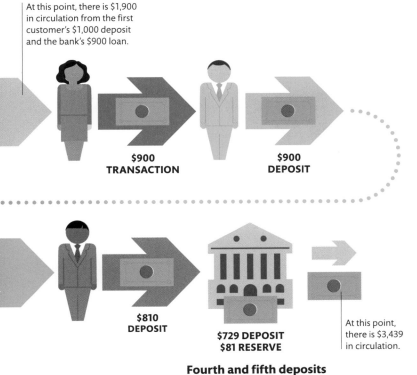

$900
TRANSACTION

$900
DEPOSIT

$810
DEPOSIT

$729 DEPOSIT
$81 RESERVE

At this point, there is $3,439 in circulation.

**Fourth and fifth deposits**
A fourth customer borrows $810, which a fifth customer returns to the bank, which keeps $81 in reserve and lends the remaining $729.

# 96%
was the amount of money held electronically in the UK by commercial banks in the form of bank deposits in 2020

www.bankofengland.co.uk

# The financial sector

The section of the economy that is made up of firms and institutions that manage money, the financial sector includes commercial and investment banks, brokers, pension funds, and insurance providers.

## The earliest banks

Many historians trace the rise of modern banking to the founding of the Medici Bank in Florence in 1397, in response to the city's burgeoning international trade. But borrowing and lending money are practices that have existed in societies across the world since the dawn of civilization, and banks—even in a more limited form—have always been there to provide people, organizations, and governments with a safe place to store money. Wherever money exists, there is a need for a system to help circulate it—as an economy evolves, a financial sector emerges.

## Financial firms and institutions

This diagram shows the main types of financial firms and institutions and the intermediary roles they play. They often engage in more than one type of intermediation—for example, commercial banks might also have investment-bank operations. In all cases, a certain level of financial risk goes hand in hand with any potential reward—a firm or institution might lose money when debts are not repaid, or are only partly repaid, or when they make the wrong investment decision.

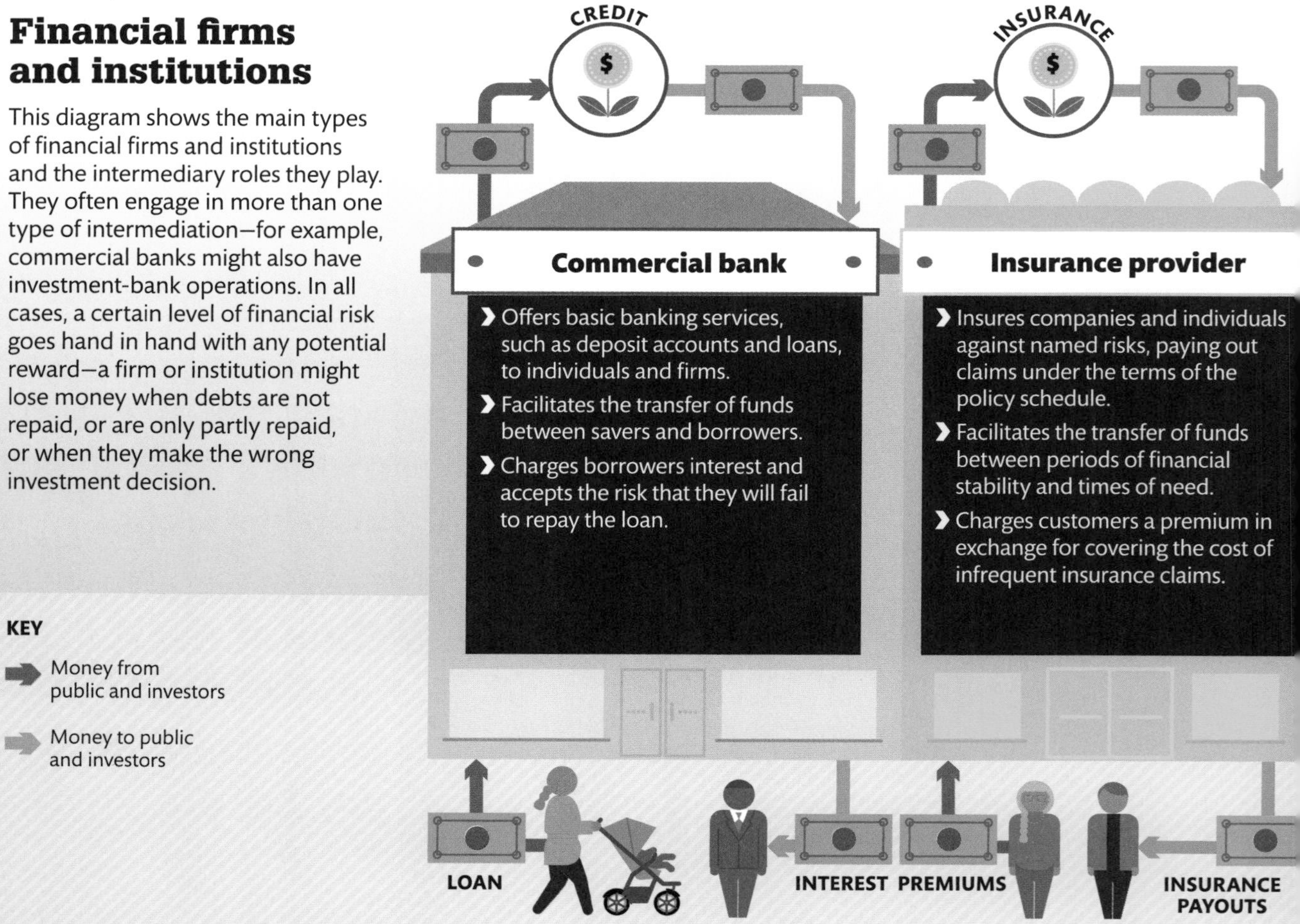

**KEY**

➡ Money from public and investors

➡ Money to public and investors

CREDIT

INSURANCE

### Commercial bank

❯ Offers basic banking services, such as deposit accounts and loans, to individuals and firms.

❯ Facilitates the transfer of funds between savers and borrowers.

❯ Charges borrowers interest and accepts the risk that they will fail to repay the loan.

### Insurance provider

❯ Insures companies and individuals against named risks, paying out claims under the terms of the policy schedule.

❯ Facilitates the transfer of funds between periods of financial stability and times of need.

❯ Charges customers a premium in exchange for covering the cost of infrequent insurance claims.

LOAN

INTEREST PREMIUMS

INSURANCE PAYOUTS

## The flow of money

The firms and institutions that make up the financial sector act as intermediaries, facilitating financial transactions between parties. They connect savers and borrowers, taking money from savers' bank deposits and investments and lending it to borrowers for mortgages and loans. Intermediation can take place over long periods of time; for example, when someone is saving for their retirement, a financial institution can help them raise funds at a time when they are capital-abundant to be used in the future, at a time when they are more capital-restricted. These firms and institutions take on some of the risk and reward incurred in the financial transactions they facilitate.

### TOO BIG TO FAIL

The term "too big to fail" encapsulates the idea that some financial firms and institutions are so large and interconnected within the global financial system that their collapse could trigger a chain reaction of events leading to a financial crash (see pp.120–121). Because these institutions are considered so important to economic stability, they are required by law to follow rules laid out by independent financial regulatory organizations. In times of crisis, governments have stepped in to bail out firms and institutions with financial assistance to prevent their collapse.

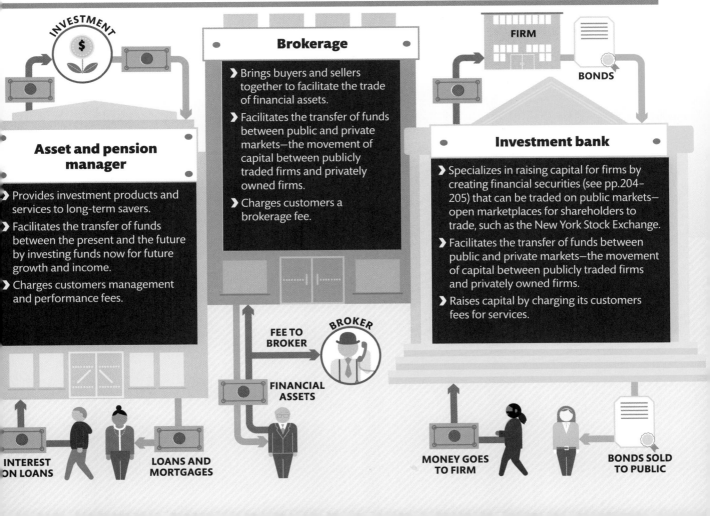

INVESTMENT

$

FIRM

BONDS

**Brokerage**

> Brings buyers and sellers together to facilitate the trade of financial assets.

> Facilitates the transfer of funds between public and private markets—the movement of capital between publicly traded firms and privately owned firms.

> Charges customers a brokerage fee.

**Asset and pension manager**

> Provides investment products and services to long-term savers.

> Facilitates the transfer of funds between the present and the future by investing funds now for future growth and income.

> Charges customers management and performance fees.

**Investment bank**

> Specializes in raising capital for firms by creating financial securities (see pp.204–205) that can be traded on public markets—open marketplaces for shareholders to trade, such as the New York Stock Exchange.

> Facilitates the transfer of funds between public and private markets—the movement of capital between publicly traded firms and privately owned firms.

> Raises capital by charging its customers fees for services.

FEE TO BROKER

BROKER

FINANCIAL ASSETS

INTEREST ON LOANS

LOANS AND MORTGAGES

MONEY GOES TO FIRM

BONDS SOLD TO PUBLIC

# Financial crashes

Signs that a financial crash is coming include a sudden drop in financial asset prices, borrowers becoming unable to repay their debts, and companies going out of business.

## The tail wagging the dog

When economies are doing well, the benefits usually spread throughout society. Businesses find demand for their products and decide to expand, consumers enjoy good wages and commit to purchases, and investors deploy capital to pursue good opportunities. During these periods, businesses, consumers, and investors may decide to take out loans to expand, consume, and invest to a greater extent than before. However, when the total amount of borrowing is too high, participants in the market can become financially vulnerable. In other words, debt may not cause a financial crash, but it can set the stage for one. Usually, the tipping point comes with the disruption of an important financial market. This can be caused by a speculative bubble bursting (see pp.200–201),

## Building to a crisis

Companies and investors deploy capital and take out loans in search of returns that compensate for risks. However, when they shift from chasing opportunities to avoiding risks, the market becomes unsettled.

### Solid foundations

When the economy is growing, people want to consume and investors deploy capital to chase financial opportunities.

> High return on capital
> Low risk aversion
> Low default rate
> Low leverage

### Cracks in the structure

Growth slows as businesses become indebted. Investors become cautious and reduce investments to minimize risk.

> High return on capital
> Low risk aversion
> Low default rate
> High leverage

a sudden spike in company default rates, a systemic banking failure, a war, or a natural disaster. In such circumstances, the disruption is only magnified when investors make decisions in a state of panic.

## Spreading panic

Disarray in the financial markets has cumulative effects throughout the economy. Panic spreads due to the forward-looking nature of financial market decisions. Investors and companies allocate capital based on the prospects of each opportunity and their confidence in future economic gains. When confidence evaporates all at once, a financial collapse ensues.

### ✓ NEED TO KNOW

❱ **Return on capital** The rate of return on financial investment opportunities. Investors seek the maximum returns and the minimum risks.

❱ **Default rate** The rate at which companies go out of business and stop repaying agreed-upon financial and contractual commitments.

❱ **Leverage** The use of borrowed money to prop up an investment strategy instead of raising money by selling financial assets such as stocks or shares.

###  CASE STUDY

#### *The crash of 2007–08*

In 2008, too much debt in the American residential sector, and the sudden failure of the Lehman Brothers investment bank, led to a crisis of confidence in financial markets worldwide. Throughout that year, many financial assets dropped in price by substantial amounts (see pp.72–73).

### Cracks become faults

Companies fail to secure new loans and start to default on their debts. Investors stop deploying capital due to increasing risks.

❱ Low return on capital
❱ High risk aversion
❱ High default rate
❱ High leverage

### Toppling down

Companies go out of business. Investors suffer permanent losses and lose confidence in the future of the economy.

# Inequality

Economic inequality—the unfair distribution of wealth and opportunity across society—can have detrimental effects on both economic growth and social cohesion.

## Unequal shares

Income and wealth are connected in two key ways: people on high incomes become wealthier than people on low incomes, and people born into wealthy families are more likely to have high-income jobs and professions, as they often grow up with better educational opportunities, networks, and resources. Poorer families are also more likely to live in rented accommodations and to depend on social welfare assistance, while richer families tend to invest money in property and receive further income from capital gains (the increase in their property's value).

As a result, unless governments restrict people from inheriting assets from their families—which most people regard as a basic right—wealth and income inequality seem to be inevitable features of societies based on liberal, free-market principles.

## Tackling inequality

One of the goals of modern politics has been to foster economic growth—which requires that people have opportunities to make money—while at the same time ensuring that people have some kind of social-security safety net. Governments that fail to do both of these

## The Gini coefficient

Income inequality is usually measured by what is known as the Gini coefficient. This measures inequality across entire populations, focusing on specific factors such as levels of income. A Gini coefficient of 0 represents perfect equality, whereas a coefficient of 1 represents perfect inequality.

GINI COEFFICIENT

0          0.5          1

### Perfect equality
In a state of perfect equality, all income values would be the same across the population. In reality, countries in northern Europe tend to have low Gini coefficients, suggesting that they are the most egalitarian societies.

### Some inequality
Most countries avoid extreme inequality, so they lie in the middle of the range. However, developing countries tend to have raised Gini coefficients, suggesting that they have more inequality than developed countries.

### Perfect inequality
In a state of perfect inequality, one individual would have all of the income. In reality, southern Africa and parts of Latin America have the highest Gini coefficients, suggesting that they have the least egalitarian societies.

risk not only social unrest, but also economic stagnation. A rise in inequality leads to fewer opportunities for the least privileged in society and therefore to an increase in household debts and default. Together, these create an unfavorable environment for firms, which produce less and hire fewer workers as demand for their goods decreases.

Structural and cultural factors can also cause inequality. A worker is effectively prohibited from switching from one labor market to another if there are no opportunities for retraining or if the price of doing so is too high. Likewise, in some occupations, workers may be discriminated against because of their gender, race, or religion. To counteract these and other problems, most governments promote job opportunities for people of all backgrounds and all income levels, and many guarantee a minimum wage—the lowest legally allowed pay for work.

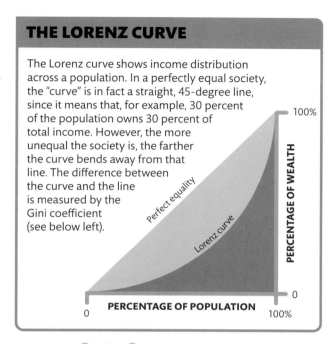

## THE LORENZ CURVE

The Lorenz curve shows income distribution across a population. In a perfectly equal society, the "curve" is in fact a straight, 45-degree line, since it means that, for example, 30 percent of the population owns 30 percent of total income. However, the more unequal the society is, the farther the curve bends away from that line. The difference between the curve and the line is measured by the Gini coefficient (see below left).

Perfect equality

Lorenz curve

PERCENTAGE OF WEALTH

100%

0

PERCENTAGE OF POPULATION

0        100%

## Wealth inequality

The distribution of wealth among adults across the world is commonly illustrated by a pyramid. This shows that in 2020, 1.1 percent of the population owned almost half (45.8 percent) of the world's total wealth, while 55 percent owned only 1.3 percent. As the global economy grows, the proportions of the middle-range groups increase, which means that global inequality decreases.

# 8.5%
## of the world's population is living on less than $2.15 a day
The World Bank (2023)

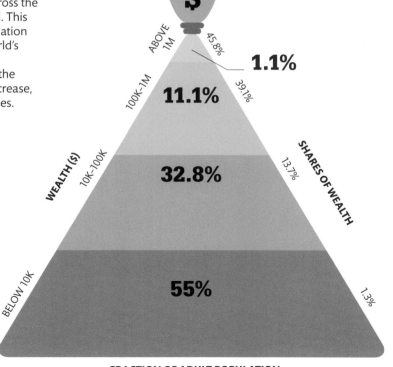

$

ABOVE 1M    45.8%    **1.1%**

100K–1M    **11.1%**    39.1%

10K–100K    **32.8%**    13.7%

WEALTH ($)    SHARES OF WEALTH

BELOW 10K    **55%**    1.3%

**FRACTION OF ADULT POPULATION**

# SCHOOLS OF ECONOMIC THOUGHT

Economists argue about how economies work—or should work. Throughout history, different "schools" of economic thought have emerged, reflecting the varying responses to issues like government intervention and financial crises.

# Classical and neoclassical economics

Today, what is known as "mainstream" or "orthodox" economic thought derives from theories that emerged in the late 18th century, a period marked by the flourishing of industry and great cultural change.

## Classical economics

In 18th-century Europe, the dominant economic theory was mercantilism, which aimed to maximize exports and minimize imports to ensure a nation's wealth. But later in the century, industrial progress brought about a deeper understanding of the economy, and, in 1776, the Scottish thinker Adam Smith (1723–1790) published *The Wealth of Nations*, which laid the foundations of what became known as classical economics. At the heart of Smith's thinking was the notion of the market—the trade of goods and services—and the concept of the "rational economic man": the idea that people base economic choices on reason and self-interest (see pp.18–19). Smith also examined the division of labor and its contribution to productivity (see pp.24–25).

## Neoclassical economics

The next generation of thinkers shifted emphasis from production as the main driver of the economy to the idea of "marginal utility"—or the preferences of the consumer (see pp.20–21). The "marginalists," led by Alfred Marshall (1842–1924), said that while producers aim to maximize profits, consumers aim to maximize utility, or satisfaction. In this way, supply and demand tends toward equilibrium. This new school of thought, known as neoclassical economics, aimed to be more rigorously scientific in its approach and is today considered the "orthodox" approach to economics.

## Changing supply and demand

Classical economics states that when demand increases, prices go up, and when supply increases, prices go down. Increased demand also leads to increased supply, but these fluctuating forces create market equilibrium.

**Demand for hot chocolate increases** as people are more likely to buy hot chocolate than ice cream in cold weather.

**THE PRICE OF HOT CHOCOLATE RISES, AS DO PROFITS**

**Hot-chocolate factory** increases production and takes on more workers.

**Outside labor force**
Those who are neither employed nor looking for a job, also known as inactive population.

**COLD WEATHER SETS IN AND IS FORECAST TO PERSIST**

## THE INVISIBLE HAND

In *The Wealth of Nations* (1776), Adam Smith explained how the self-interest of buyers and sellers in the market leads to a system that balances supply and demand and determines the price of goods and services. It is, he said, as if an "invisible hand" is guiding the process, and, in this way, the economy functions best when left to regulate itself. Smith did, however, recognize that a market economy also had its flaws—for example, in the provision of public goods and services. He believed that governments have a vital role to play in overcoming these market failures, as well as providing a legal framework to ensure the smooth working of the market.

**Demand for ice cream falls**
as people are less likely to buy ice cream than hot chocolate in cold weather.

"It is the aim of good government to stimulate production, of bad government to encourage consumption."

Jean-Baptiste Say, 18th-century French economist, *A Treatise On Political Economy* (1803)

**THE PRICE OF ICE CREAM FALLS, AS DO PROFITS**

**WORKERS CHANGE JOBS**

**Ice-cream factory**
cuts back production and number of workers.

CLOSED

# Keynesian economics

British economist John Maynard Keynes argued that, instead of leaving markets to determine themselves, governments should occasionally manage them with fiscal and monetary policies.

## Chains of spending

John Maynard Keynes (1883–1946) developed his ideas in the 1930s, during the time of the Great Depression. He questioned the assumption that economies should be left alone to correct themselves in times of crisis and argued instead that governments should intervene in the economy, particularly during recessions (see pp.94–95). He published his ideas in *The General Theory of Employment, Interest and Money*, which challenged the belief that free markets, which run themselves, ensure full employment.

Keynes argued that wages and prices are "sticky"—that is, they do not automatically fall when there is a fall in demand for labor—and that because of this, demand for labor decreases further, which leads to unemployment. Economic activity, he claimed, is determined by demand— that is, by the amount of spending in the economy—and when this falls beneath a certain level, it causes high unemployment. Furthermore, "sticky" wages and labor costs prevent this from being remedied by the markets alone.

According to Keynes, the only remedy is state intervention— in particular, the injection of money into the economy by the government to increase demand. Such injections trigger chains of spending that run throughout the economy and multiply the value of the government's initial outlay. Today, this is known as the government "spending its way out of a recession."

**Government investment**

Instead of reducing its spending, the government can inject money directly into the economy. It can do so by creating jobs, which will stimulate production and increase demand.

## THE KEYNESIAN MULTIPLIER

The mechanism whereby governments spend money to increase demand, which in turn increases supply, is known as the "Keynesian multiplier." If, for example, the government injects $100 billion into the economy, and people spend 80 percent of that money on goods (and save the rest), $80 billion becomes additional income for the people who produced those goods—and if they spend 80 percent of that income on other goods, the producers of those other goods receive $64 billion dollars of extra income, and so on. After ten rounds of this, the initial $100 billion could turn into more than $500 billion worth of spending throughout the economy.

## Stimulating the economy

According to Keynes, when economic growth slows down, an injection of money can provide the stimulus for recovery. The initial investment kick-starts a chain of spending and production, which increases the circulation of money throughout the economy and promotes further economic activity.

## Infrastructure

One way that a government can put money into the economy is by investing it in infrastructure—for example, by building houses or modernizing roads and power supplies.

> "All production **is for the purpose of** ultimately satisfying a consumer."

John Maynard Keynes, *The General Theory of Employment, Interest and Money* (1936)

## Increased spending

Government spending stimulates industry, which increases the number of workers with disposable incomes. This in turn leads to a greater demand for goods and services.

## Further circulation of money

Stimulated by an initial injection of government money, activity in the economy accelerates. This brings more money into circulation.

## Increased production

Businesses respond to the rise in demand by increasing production. This increases profits, creates jobs, raises wages, and stimulates further investment.

**WAGES**

**GOODS**

**INVESTMENT**

## A healthy economy

The government's initial outlay has multiplied the production of goods and services. It has also increased employment and wages and promoted investment in industry.

# Post-Keynesian economics

In the 1970s, a group of Keynesian economists challenged the more orthodox, free-market policies that were gaining prominence in Europe and the United States.

## Effective demand

The "post-Keynesian" school of economics took its inspiration not only from John Maynard Keynes (see pp.128–129), but also from many Marxian (see pp.132–133) and neo-Ricardian (see pp.158–159) economists. The school flourished in the UK and the US, where it opposed what became known as the "neoliberal," supply-side economics that were being introduced there (see pp.140–141). Instead, post-Keynesians, such as Hyman Minsky (see box) and others, promoted the principle of "effective demand," which stated that governments should intervene in the economy to boost demand instead of supply. They also argued that full employment cannot be brought about by market forces alone, which, if left unregulated, perpetuate the cycle of "boom and bust."

## Predicting a crash

In their critique of neoliberal economics, the post-Keynesians stressed that deregulating the financial sector increased the risk of a financial crash (see pp.120–121). Their predictions proved to be correct: overconfidence in a booming economy, combined with poorly regulated financial markets, led to a global financial crash in 2007–2008 (see pp.72–73). In the wake of this crisis, many of the countries that had promoted neoliberal policies turned to post-Keynesian economics to hasten recovery.

## Stabilizing an economy

Free-market economies have business cycles that rise and fall periodically (see pp.90–91) and occasionally fluctuate between extremes of prosperity ("boom") and bankruptcy ("bust"). Post-Keynesian economists identified several measures that could prevent this instability, or at least avoid its most damaging effects.

### Stimulating demand

The government should stimulate demand instead of supply—for example, by cutting taxes for consumers instead of businesses.

### Addressing inequality

Reducing inequality puts money fairly in the pockets of the largest proportion of people, whose spending increases demand.

## THE "MINSKY MOMENT"

Hyman Minsky (1919–1996) studied how economies expand and contract. He noted that during periods of rising prosperity, levels of both speculative investment and debt often increase without corresponding increases in cash flow. In such circumstances, when debt exceeds the amount of money that borrowers can repay, the lending supply stops and the economy abruptly contracts.

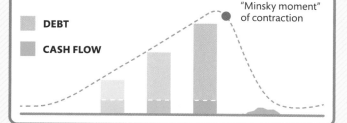

■ DEBT

■ CASH FLOW

"Minsky moment" of contraction

### Regulating financial institutions

The financial sector should be properly regulated to prevent investors and traders from making fortunes at the expense of the country's economic security.

# "An increase in the number of paupers does not broaden the market."

Michał Kalecki, Polish Marxian economist,
*Theory of Economic Dynamics* (1965)

### Lender of last resort

If a financial institution runs out of money, a lender of last resort, such as a central bank, should bail it out to prevent a financial panic.

# Marxian economics

One of the most influential thinkers of the 19th century, Karl Marx founded a school of economic thought that provided a critique of capitalism and a radical socialist alternative.

### A critique of capitalism

Although widely regarded as a revolutionary thinker, Karl Marx (1818–1883) began writing within the tradition of classical economics. In his three-volume critique of capitalism, *Das Kapital* (1867–1894), he took the classical view that production, instead of exchange or consumption, is the cornerstone of the economy and that society is divided into distinct economic classes. For Marx, capitalist society consists of two of these classes: the bourgeoisie (the capitalist owners of industry) and the proletariat (the workers who provide the labor). He believed that the bourgeoisie make their profits from the surplus value produced by the proletariat and that measures to increase productivity, such as division of labor or increased mechanization, have a detrimental, or alienating, effect on the workers.

### Class struggle

Marx argued that although capitalism has been successful in driving economic growth, it is

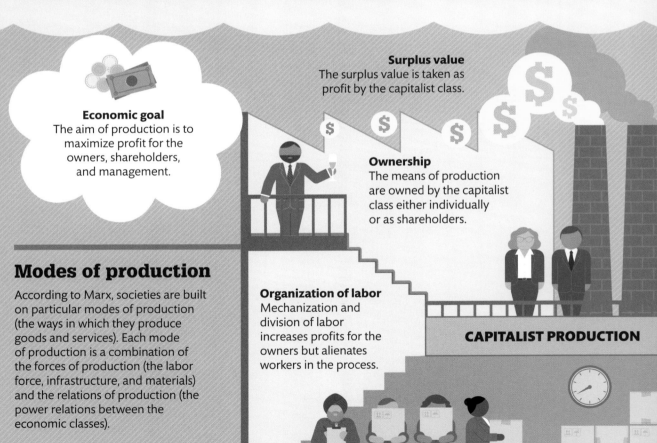

**Economic goal**
The aim of production is to maximize profit for the owners, shareholders, and management.

**Surplus value**
The surplus value is taken as profit by the capitalist class.

**Ownership**
The means of production are owned by the capitalist class either individually or as shareholders.

## Modes of production

According to Marx, societies are built on particular modes of production (the ways in which they produce goods and services). Each mode of production is a combination of the forces of production (the labor force, infrastructure, and materials) and the relations of production (the power relations between the economic classes).

**Organization of labor**
Mechanization and division of labor increases profits for the owners but alienates workers in the process.

**CAPITALIST PRODUCTION**

untenable in the longer term. He claimed that throughout history economic systems have changed due to conflict between the classes and that capitalism will ultimately be swept away by a socialist revolution. After this, the proletariat will own the means of production and will benefit collectively from the surplus value. According to Marx, because the capitalist market economy is inherently unstable, its boom-and-bust fluctuations will lead to its own demise. After that, under a socialist government, a central authority will provide a stable alternative to market-based economics.

## "From each according to his abilities, to each according to his needs."

Karl Marx, *The Criticism of the Gotha Programme* (1875)

## COMMUNISM

During the 20th century, a number of countries adopted a radical form of Marxian economics known as "communism." These included the Soviet Union and China and nations such as Cuba, North Korea, and several newly independent African republics. However, capitalism did not end as Marx predicted, but consistently outperformed the communist economies, most of which later collapsed.

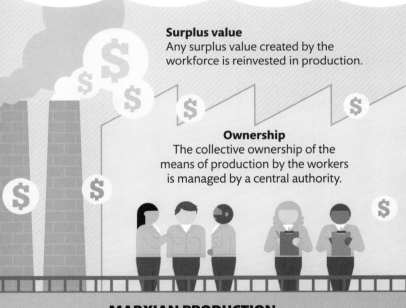

**Surplus value**
Any surplus value created by the workforce is reinvested in production.

**Ownership**
The collective ownership of the means of production by the workers is managed by a central authority.

**Economic goal**
The aim of production is to provide goods and services for the people.

### MARXIAN PRODUCTION

**Organization of labor**
Workers participate in all aspects of production, take pride in their work, and share their wealth.

## ✓ NEED TO KNOW

› **Surplus value** The difference between the price of a commodity on the market and the amount it cost to produce it.
› **Labor theory of value** According to Marx, the economic value of a commodity should not be measured by the market but by the amount of labor that went into producing it.

# Schumpeterian economics

**According to Schumpeterian economics, capitalist economies are not static, but dynamic and continually evolving, driven by innovations that force out inefficient businesses to make way for new growth.**

## Innovation and growth

Named after Moravian-born American economist Joseph Schumpeter (1883–1950), Schumpeterian economics, like Marxian economics (see pp.132–133), places great emphasis on technological development as a feature of capitalist economies. Schumpeter, however, went further by arguing that economic growth, including advances in technology, is driven more by innovation—entrepreneurs promoting new ideas and products that not only reap rewards, but also create the atmosphere for change.

The introduction of a new product encourages other firms to do the same, finding new ways to increase productivity and driving advances in technology. This in turn makes the product cheaper and more widely available, but also less profitable—so older companies,

## "A depression is for capitalism like a good, cold douche."

Joseph Schumpeter, to economics students, recorded by
R. L. Heilbroner, *The Worldly Philosophers* (1953)

## Innovation cycles

At the heart of Schumpeter's analysis of the capitalist economy is the idea of innovation cycles. A cycle starts with a new product, prompting competition, which in turn fosters technological progress. Less productive firms fail, leaving more productive companies to benefit—and from them a new wave of innovative entrepreneurs emerges.

### 1. Innovation

An entrepreneur introduces a new product, such as the first camera, to the market. The firm launching this product initially makes a high profit from the innovation.

### 2. Competition

Other firms start to produce cameras, competing for a share of the market. Competition means prices fall, making the product less profitable. However, constant innovation feeds consumer demand for new cameras.

if they cannot modernize, eventually fail. Over time, the market for the new product settles and even stagnates, prompting a new generation of entrepreneurs to come up with further innovations.

## "Creative destruction"

The idea of innovation driving technological advance and economic growth contrasted with the established neoclassical theory (see pp.126–127) of supply and demand allocating resources to the market efficiently and maintaining equilibrium (see pp.104–105). Instead, Schumpeter saw the capitalist economy as an evolutionary process of continuous innovation and "creative destruction." He even suggested that recessions (see pp.94–95) are a necessary part of the capitalist system to weed out inefficiency and allow dynamic innovation and growth.

## CASE STUDY

### Sound recording

The sound-recording industry is an example of Schumpeterian economics in practice. From the initial innovation of recording sound on wax cylinders in the 1870s, the industry has progressed through gramophone records and vinyl discs, to tape cassettes and CDs, to MP3 downloads and web-based streaming. At each stage, the brands that drove the innovations—such as the Edison Phonograph Company, RCA Victor, EMI, and Sony Walkman—dominated the market but then all but disappeared as new technologies rendered their products obsolete.

### 3. Destruction and progress

In a competitive market, some firms inevitably fail, while others thrive. This drives rival firms to become more productive, spurring new development and technological advances.

### 4. Economic renewal

As less dynamic firms fail, others become market leaders. Their profits grow, allowing them to further increase productivity and also drive the development of new products, such as the digital camera.

### 5. Cycle repeats

A new generation of innovative entrepreneurs takes advantage of the technological advances and comes up with new ideas, such as the touchscreen phone with built-in camera, so the cycle begins once again.

# Institutional economics

**A small but influential school of economic thought that emerged in the US in the early 20th century, institutional economics focuses on the ways in which social and cultural phenomena shape economic behavior.**

## A sociological approach

Influenced by the comparatively new discipline of sociology, this approach to economics examined the connections between economic actors (firms and individuals) and the various "institutions" of society, from the formal institutions of the state—such as its government and laws—to its less formal traditions, customs, and culture. Thorstein Veblen (1857–1929), regarded as the founding father of institutional economics, illustrated the theory in his 1899 book, *The Theory of the Leisure Class*. In this, he described the "conspicuous consumption"—buying in order to impress—of the nouveau riche. At the same time, firms tried to create demand for their products instead of provide what consumers needed in order to maximize profits and gain power.

## Social and political power

Among Veblen's followers was John Commons (1862–1945), who advised that governments should act as mediators between firms and consumers. The idea was taken up by John Kenneth Galbraith (1908–2006), who believed the economy had become so dominated by big firms that consumers were no longer acting in their own best interests. Large firms also wielded political power, influencing government policies in their favor. To overcome this imbalance of power, he advocated government intervention, including price control, and the nationalization of public services and key industries.

> ## "We are not smart enough to leave things to the market."
>
> Ha-Joon Chang, *23 Things They Don't Tell You About Capitalism* (2010)

## INCOMPATIBLE INSTITUTIONS

International trade relies on the various resources, goods, services, and needs of different countries, but differences in their institutions can sometimes pose a problem for firms. Laws—not only those governing imports and exports, but also things such as safety standards and food regulations—vary from place to place, and even social conventions may have a bearing on what can and cannot be traded.

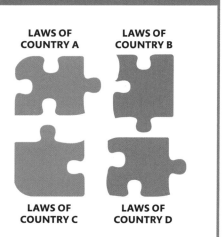

LAWS OF COUNTRY A

LAWS OF COUNTRY B

LAWS OF COUNTRY C

LAWS OF COUNTRY D

## How firms keep consumers coming back for more

Institutional economists argue that firms often profit from cultural customs—for example, the desire to have the latest up-to-date gadget. To boost sales, the firm releases an updated version of a device, declaring that it makes earlier versions redundant; the consumer literally buys into the idea that it is the latest thing, a "must-have" item, regardless of its actual usefulness. This practice of designing products to have a limited useful life is known as "planned obsolescence."

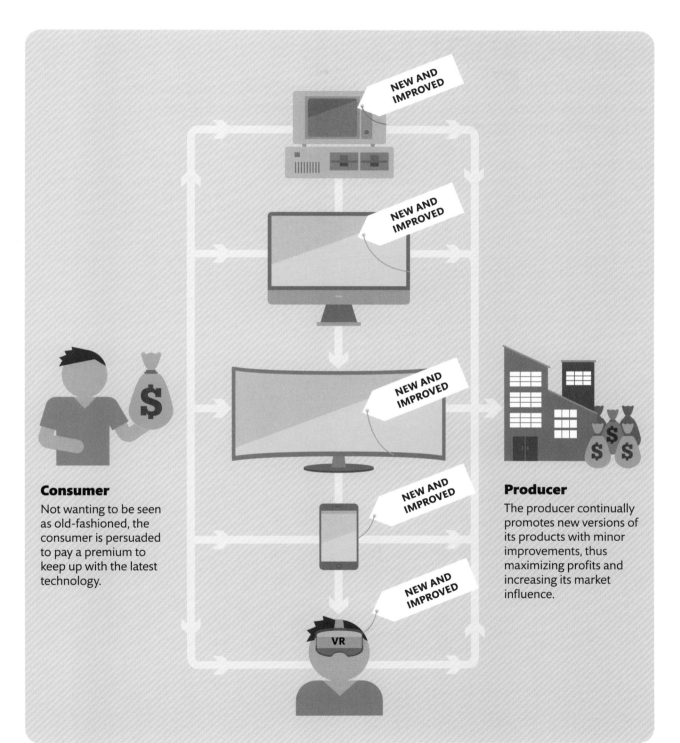

**NEW AND IMPROVED**

**NEW AND IMPROVED**

**NEW AND IMPROVED**

**NEW AND IMPROVED**

**NEW AND IMPROVED**

VR

**Consumer**

Not wanting to be seen as old-fashioned, the consumer is persuaded to pay a premium to keep up with the latest technology.

**Producer**

The producer continually promotes new versions of its products with minor improvements, thus maximizing profits and increasing its market influence.

# The Austrian School

In the late 19th century, a group of Austrian economists broke away from neoclassical and Marxian economics in favor of a model driven by the economic choices of individuals.

## The individual is key

In the 19th century, neoclassical (see pp.126–127) and Marxian (see pp.132–133) economists set out "scientific" explanations for the workings of the economy. The Austrian School rejected these principles, harking back to classical ideas of individual freedom. It believed the economy to be the result of individuals' actions, based on their personal knowledge, experience, expectations, and motivations. The economy functions best, therefore, when individuals are free to make their own choices. Economic restrictions from the state are coercive and aren't compatible with ideals of political freedom.

## The Austrian legacy

The first economists of the Austrian School, such as Carl Menger (1840–1921), Eugen von Böhm-Bawerk (1851–1914), and Friedrich von Wieser (1851–1926), were considered outside mainstream thought. However, many of their ideas have been accepted into "orthodox" economics. They all concern issues of individual preference and motivation. For example, marginal utility (see pp.20–21) is the value gained by someone from consuming one more unit of an item.

## The problem with central planning

Economists of the Austrian School were implacably opposed to the Marxian idea of a centrally planned economy. Because market prices provide information about value, a central planner will always lack enough information to make good decisions about how much to produce and how much to charge consumers for it.

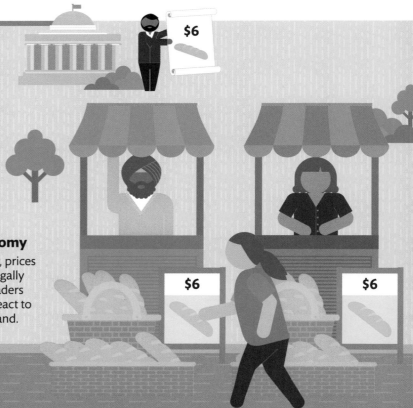

### A centrally planned economy

In a centrally planned economy, prices are set by the state. Prices are legally fixed for a specific period, so traders have no flexibility and cannot react to fluctuations in supply and demand.

Opportunity cost (see pp.22–23) describes the trade-offs made when choosing one action over another. Time preference theory (see pp.76–77) discusses the time in considering the value of an item. It suggests that individuals typically prefer present benefits to future benefits. A second generation of Austrian economists, led by

Ludwig von Mises (1881–1973), continued to challenge neoclassical orthodoxy, as well as centrally planned economies (see below), which were proposed by Marx. Friedrich Hayek's (1899–1992) pragmatic interpretation of the Austrian School influenced the development of neoliberalism (see pp.140–141).

## THE SUBJECTIVE THEORY OF VALUE

The Austrian School's subjective theory of value challenged the established idea that an item's value is determined by an objective assessment of its worth based on how much it cost to produce. It argues that value depends on the preferences of the individuals buying and selling the item and that this value can fluctuate over time as perceptions of usefulness or desirability change. Therefore, the role of consumers is key: without price signals from the market, decisions about what and how much to supply cannot be made in the most efficient way.

"**The more the state 'plans,' the more difficult planning becomes for the individual.**"

Friedrich Hayek, *The Road to Serfdom* (1944)

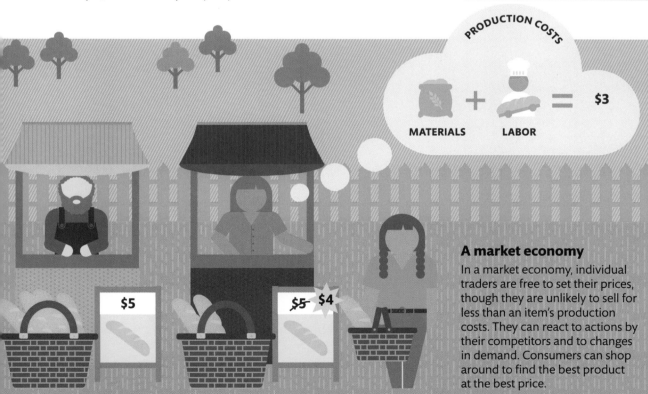

PRODUCTION COSTS

MATERIALS + LABOR = $3

$5

$5 $4

### A market economy

In a market economy, individual traders are free to set their prices, though they are unlikely to sell for less than an item's production costs. They can react to actions by their competitors and to changes in demand. Consumers can shop around to find the best product at the best price.

# Neoliberalism

**The doctrine of neoliberalism, which came of age in the 1990s, has its roots in the theories of Austrian economists Ludwig von Mises and Friedrich Hayek.**

## Rolling back the state

After witnessing the ravaging effects of various totalitarian regimes—including fascism, Nazism, and Soviet communism—Ludwig von Mises (1881–1973) and Friedrich Hayek (1899–1992) concluded that prosperity and freedom could only be guaranteed by limiting government powers.

Mises proposed the opposite of state control. He argued that governments should have no say in the markets, which should be left alone to determine distribution and prices, and that individuals should be given complete economic freedom to act as they see fit. Hayek took this idea a step further, suggesting that governments do have a role to play in the economy, but only in promoting policies that encourage economic growth and removing obstacles to the freedom of individuals to make their own economic decisions.

After World War II (1939–1945), Mises' and Hayek's ideas became popular in the anticommunist and libertarian politics of the US, and Milton Friedman (1912–2006) emerged as a key influence on neoliberal thought.

## Freeing the market

In agreement with Hayek, Friedman believed that economic growth was crucial to economic success and argued that governments should foster this by lowering taxes, reducing business regulations, and enabling free trade instead of trying to manage demand. At first, neoliberalism—as it came to be known—gained little support in a world that was dominated by neoclassical theory. However, since its adoption by Margaret Thatcher in the UK and Ronald Reagan in the US in the 1980s, it has been embraced enthusiastically across the world.

## LAFFER CURVE

On a graph now known as the Laffer Curve, American economist Arthur Laffer (b. 1940) demonstrated that at a certain point, increasing taxation rates results in a fall in revenue for the government. His findings added support for the neoliberal policy of cutting taxes.

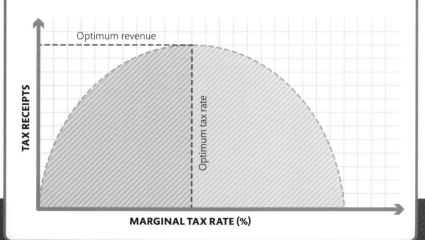

Optimum revenue

Optimum tax rate

TAX RECEIPTS

MARGINAL TAX RATE (%)

"There is no such thing as public money; there is only taxpayers' money."

**Margaret Thatcher, British Prime Minister (1983)**

# Fostering growth

Central to the neoliberal philosophy is the idea that to foster economic growth, members of the entrepreneurial class should be allowed to thrive and to increase their wealth. This will ultimately benefit the wider population, because that wealth then trickles down through the economy to the poor in the form of increased spending, investment in industry, the creation of new or better jobs, and a better standard of living as a whole.

### Releasing money

Lowering tax rates acts as an incentive to entrepreneurs and businesses to innovate and expand. It also enables the wealthy to invest their money in flourishing new businesses.

### Money flows

The more businesses flourish, the more jobs become available and the more people become employed. This in turn improves the supply of goods and services and creates more jobs.

### Money makes money

As the economy grows, people have more money to spend, which in turn increases demand. This leads to more and better job opportunities and increased standards of living.

# Environmental economics

In recent decades, economists have looked for new, sustainable ways in which nations can manage their resources and avoid the environmental damage that often comes with economic development.

## Costing the Earth?

Most economists argue that economic progress over the last few centuries has caused harm to the environment (from the depletion of its natural resources to climate change). They also agree that, left unchecked, these issues will also have a potentially catastrophic economic impact.

In light of this, many economists propose a fundamentally different way of thinking about economics—reframing economics as an aspect of the environment instead of the conventional view of the environment as an aspect of economics. They argue that the success of an economy is dependent on careful stewardship of the natural world.

## A greener world

While scientists work on developing new technologies to mitigate the effects of climate change, governments around the world are incentivizing people to live and work more sustainably and to switch to renewable sources of energy.

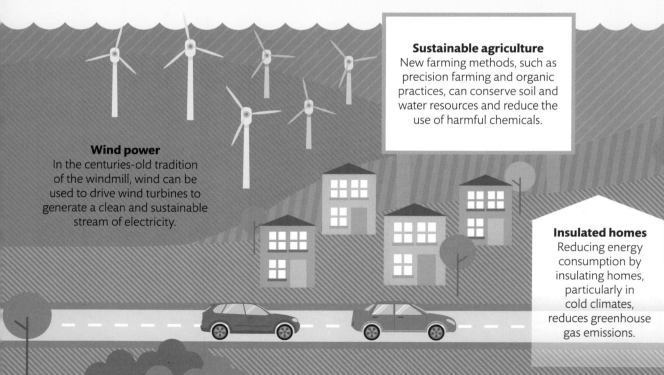

**Sustainable agriculture**
New farming methods, such as precision farming and organic practices, can conserve soil and water resources and reduce the use of harmful chemicals.

**Wind power**
In the centuries-old tradition of the windmill, wind can be used to drive wind turbines to generate a clean and sustainable stream of electricity.

**Insulated homes**
Reducing energy consumption by insulating homes, particularly in cold climates, reduces greenhouse gas emissions.

## Sustainability

The core idea at the heart of environmental economics is that of a focus on sustainability instead of the growth-and-profit model favored by free-market economics and the *laissez-faire* system (see pp.126–127). Environmental economists argue that environmental damage should actually be considered a market failure (see pp.36–37) and that governments should therefore intervene to prevent it. Such measures might include green taxes, fines for pollution, or carbon trading; however, because the crisis is global, they will require more international cooperation (see box). Some critics have also raised concerns that such measures do not go far enough to save the environment or offer a genuinely sustainable economic model.

### THE PARIS AGREEMENT

In 2015, 196 countries negotiated a treaty on climate change at the United Nations Climate Change Conference in Paris, France. Known as the Paris Agreement, the treaty committed its signatories to keeping "the increase in the global average temperature to well below 3.6°F (2°C) above preindustrial levels"—which they have done by implementing economic policies aimed at reducing greenhouse gas emissions. However, to meet the target, emissions must have declined by 43 percent by 2030, which is by no means guaranteed. Although there is no clear way to enforce the agreement, its parties are legally bound to have their progress tracked by experts.

# 1.2bn people could be displaced by climate change and civil unrest by 2050

Institute for Economics & Peace (2020)

**Tidal power**
Coastal areas and islands can harness the ebb and flow of the oceans to provide clean electricity.

**Solar power**
Sunlight can be converted into electricity via solar panels, which can be mounted on roofs or installed in designated solar "farms."

**Electric vehicles (EVs)**
The adoption of electric vehicles is on the rise. As technology advances and economies of scale kick in, EVs are likely to become more affordable and accessible.

# Well-being economics

The health of a nation's economy is normally judged in financial terms, but the well-being economy proposes a new approach in which economic policy focuses on social well-being and environmental health.

## Redefining success

Economics has traditionally been concerned with production, consumption, and wealth and has measured success with indicators such as GDP (see pp.88–89). Well-being economists do not dismiss the importance of financial prosperity, but they argue for a broader measure of success and economic policies. The well-being of people and the planet should drive economic policy instead of be an afterthought. The standard of living index, productivity figures, and how wealth is distributed provide some detail, but other aspects of society need to be examined.

## Measuring quality of life

It is not straightforward to assess the well-being of a nation. Multiple factors determine quality of life. While some, such as life expectancy and education, are measurable, others are less quantifiable and may be based more on opinions than facts.

### Healthy environment

A healthy society needs clean air, drinking water, fresh food, healthy accommodations, safe working environments, adequate public transportation, green spaces, and bike paths.

### A sense of social belonging

People should feel included in the political process, both locally and nationally. Community centers, local organizations, clubs, and faith groups help foster a sense of community.

### Opportunities for recreation

Leisure activities contribute to well-being. There should be suitable provision of sports and other recreational facilities, venues for arts and entertainment, parks, and libraries.

### Universal education

Literacy and numeracy levels are indicators of educational standards, as are the provision of state-funded education for all children and a range of colleges and universities.

Existing indices of national well-being include the Physical Quality of Life Index, based on basic literacy, infant mortality, and life expectancy; the Human Development Index (see p.87), used in the United Nations' Human Development Report; and more recently, the Happy Planet Index, which incorporates a measure of a nation's ecological footprint.

## Gross National Happiness

Probably the best-known attempt to provide an alternative to GDP as a measure of a nation's well-being was undertaken in Bhutan in the late 1970s. A comparatively poor country, it introduced Gross National Happiness—a scale on which it scored more highly than many much wealthier countries.

# DOUGHNUT ECONOMICS

In *Doughnut Economics* (2017), British economist Kate Raworth (b. 1970) presented a model for promoting more socially just and environmentally sustainable economies. A green "doughnut" shape represents the conditions under which humanity can thrive. Around it are boundaries marking the social and environmental limits for sustainable economic development. The internal orange area lacks life's essentials, such as food, water, and shelter. Around the outside, Earth's life-support systems, such as soil, biodiversity, and pollution, are degraded beyond repair.

## "Life, Liberty and the pursuit of Happiness."

**The US Declaration of Independence (1776)**

## Freedoms of belief and speech

Fundamental human and civil rights, protected by law, contribute to a satisfactory quality of life, including the right to free speech and the protection of religious and political beliefs.

## Mental healthcare

The way a nation looks after its less fortunate— for example, those dealing with mental health issues, abuse, or unemployment— demonstrates how caring a society is.

## Physical healthcare

Factors such as life expectancy, universal healthcare, and the ratio of healthcare professionals to the population are all indicators of a nation's healthcare provision.

## Rewarding employment

Job satisfaction requires material rewards, like a realistic living wage, but also measures such as job security, pension provision, union membership, and feeling valued as an employee.

# Behavioral economics

Since the mid-20th century, economists have looked to the field of psychology to help them better understand how people make economic decisions in real-world situations.

## Bounded rationality

A key concept in classical economics is that of *Homo economicus*—the ideal individual who makes entirely rational economic decisions (see pp.18–19). However, in the 1940s, Herbert Simon (1916–2001) questioned the usefulness of such a concept; he argued that an individual's ability to act rationally is restricted, in the sense that situations are often complex and uncertain, which can make it hard to reach a rational conclusion, particularly given limited information. The alternative is not that humans act irrationally, but that they act with what Simon called "bounded rationality"—that is, using shortcuts, such as identifying patterns and restricting options. Simon also argued that bounded rationality applies as much to organizations and institutions as it does to individuals.

## Forms of cognitive bias

Individuals tend to judge situations using heuristics (rules of thumb), so they are sometimes prone to jumping to unjustified conclusions. Such conclusions, and any decisions based on them, are based not on actual probabilities, but instead on an assessment of incomplete information. This "cognitive bias," as Kahneman calls it, can take a number of different forms.

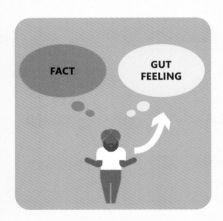

**Neglect of probability**
When an individual is confronted with a difficult decision, they may go with their gut feeling and ignore the available information.

**The bandwagon effect**
Individuals often rely on the opinions of others, deciding on a course of action simply because a lot of people believe it is correct.

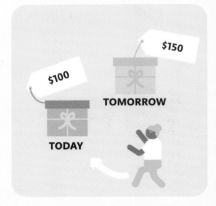

**Hyperbolic discounting**
An individual's decision may be influenced by the temptation of an immediate reward instead of a better outcome in the long term.

## Rules of thumb

Simon's idea was adopted by psychologists Amos Tversky (1937–1996) and Daniel Kahneman (1934–), who examined the decision-making process. Like Simon, they found that in situations involving risk and uncertainty, the conventional theory that people act rationally was incorrect. In practice, people generally base their decisions on heuristics, or "rules of thumb," which give them a rough idea of probable outcomes.

However, Tversky and Kahneman also noticed that heuristic thinking is biased. For example, people often overestimate the probability of unlikely things happening (such as winning the lottery) and underestimate the probability of more likely things happening (such as becoming injured while playing a dangerous sport).

### THINKING FAST AND THINKING SLOW

Tversky and Kahneman argued that human beings have two distinct decision-making processes: "thinking fast" and "thinking slow." While people should ideally use logic to deliberate consciously and slowly, they often have limited time and information, so they have to react quickly to a situation. This is an automatic response involving minimal conscious evaluation and relies on rules of thumb that are based on insufficient information and often false assumptions. Understanding the extent to which people think fast instead of slow has enabled economists to better model the way people assess companies and make investments.

"Economists **think about what people** ought to do. Psychologists **watch what they** actually do."

Daniel Kahneman, Israeli-American psychologist and economist

### Anchoring
Individuals sometimes rely entirely on a single piece of information and remain ignorant of all other relevant considerations.

### The framing effect
The way options are presented, either positively or negatively, can affect an individual's judgment when making a decision.

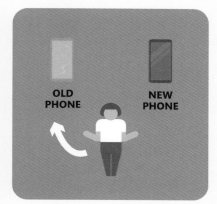

### The status quo bias
When faced with a difficult decision, individuals often opt for the familiarity of the way things are instead of risk making a change.

# Complexity and chaos

Until recently, economists believed that economies could be modeled according to simple, mechanical rules. However, economies are like people—they are extremely complex and often behave in unpredictable ways.

## A simple machine?

Since the time of Adam Smith (see pp.126–127), economists have tried to make their work as scientific as possible, basing their theories on objective facts instead of conjecture. For this reason, they have tended to assume that economies, like efficient machines, behave in ways that can be predicted.

However, in practice, real-world economies are complex, involving numerous interconnected elements, and operate in ways that do not fit neatly into any economic theory. Individuals often act in unexpected ways (see pp.146–147), and unforeseen events, such as natural disasters, can have huge effects on economic systems.

## A complex system

None of the variables in an economy exists in isolation. A firm that produces goods and services interacts with other firms—including suppliers of materials—as well as with financial institutions, such as banks, and with the households that consume its products. Together, these variables form a complex, interconnected economic network.

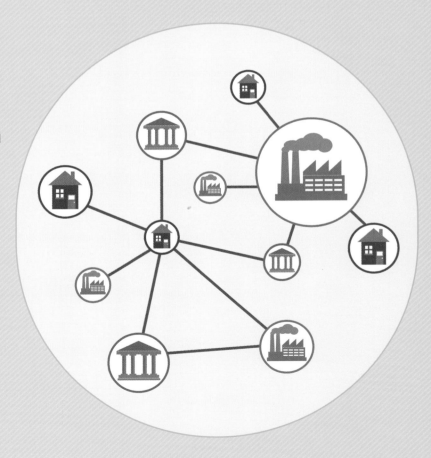

### A LINKED SYSTEM

The actions of any agent (firm, household, or financial institution) in the economy will have effects on other agents with whom they are directly connected. This in turn affects the prosperity of others in more distant parts of the network.

## Complexity economics

Toward the end of the 20th century, economists began to realize that their mechanistic model of the economy was naive. At the same time, a new field of research, known as "complexity theory," was showing that seemingly insignificant actions can cause chains of events that have increasingly unpredictable effects. Although it began in meteorology, complexity theory soon gave rise to "complexity economics," which studies the ways in which economies are not only complex and dynamic, but often as unpredictable as the weather. This new approach has cast doubt over many traditional theories in economics and has shown how—and why—it is difficult to model such complex systems as stock markets and foreign exchanges.

"**Complexity economics sees the economy [...] as organic, always creating itself, alive and full of messy vitality.**"

W. Brian Arthur, Northern Irish economist, "Foundations of complexity economics," *Nature Reviews* (2021)

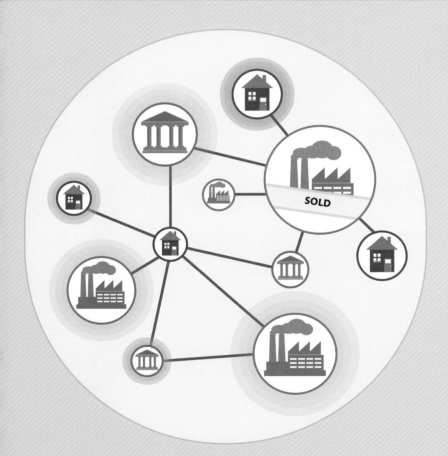

### FEEDBACK AND OSCILLATIONS

In complex systems, the process of action and reaction can generate extreme or chaotic outcomes. A circular chain of cause and effect, known as a "feedback loop," may be initiated by a small transaction and snowball into a major event, such as a run on a bank. Complex systems also "oscillate" from one state to another as they move out of steady states. In economics, the "boom and bust" cycle is a classic example of oscillation (see pp.90–91).

### RIPPLE EFFECT

A change, such as when a firm is sold, has an impact on everyone who has dealings with the firm. The new owners may change suppliers, attract new customers, or encourage more investors. In this way, the change causes ripples throughout the whole economy.

# Feminist economics

Historically, society and the study of economics have been dominated by men, so the role of women in economic affairs has been undervalued or even ignored. Feminist economics seeks to address this imbalance.

## A feminist perspective

In the 20th century, feminism gained considerable momentum, forcing a reevaluation of women's role in all aspects of society. Economics was no exception, and a growing body of feminist economists pointed out the inherent biases in the management and study of the economy. Ever since, feminist economics has argued that these biases stem from cultural gender stereotypes. These lead to biases toward traditionally "male" characteristics, such as self-interest, competitiveness, and risk-taking, while downplaying "feminine" characteristics, such as empathy, altruism, and cooperation.

Feminist economics challenges the orthodox model of all-powerful markets operated by rationally self-interested agents (see pp.18–19). It argues that, instead of reflecting reality, such a model simply promotes those characteristics, further increasing inequity and gender bias. Feminist economists propose alternative methods of measuring economic success and a reappraisal of women's role in the economy.

## A woman's place

One of the glaring injustices of conventional economics is the undervaluing of women's contribution to the economy. Women have been effectively excluded from positions of economic power and instead restricted to traditionally "female" occupations, typically in the service sector or in menial work, which are generally poorly paid. A large proportion of the female workforce is even unpaid, remaining at home to care for dependent families. In this way, society benefits from the resource of a large pool of cheap or free labor.

## The need for a new perspective

In order to address the structural problems of inequality, feminist economists call for a comprehensive approach that encompasses equal pay, revaluing traditionally female-dominated work, reducing unpaid labor burdens, and empowering women in leadership positions.

### Gender-balanced leadership
> Promote policies that train, mentor, and recruit women into leadership positions to give them more power to influence change.
> Change work culture, such as flexible working and reformed childcare, so women can be more economically active.

### Addressing pay inequality
> Implement and enforce laws that require equal pay for equal work.
> Support transparency in salary information to identify and address wage gaps.
> Enforce firms to regularly report gender pay gap data.

### Combating undervalued work
> Encourage efforts to break down gender-based roles in work, including hiring women into underrepresented roles.
> Revalue the contribution of traditionally "female" work and pay workers fairly based on their contribution.

### Addressing unpaid work
> Promote polices such as paid family leave and affordable childcare so that individuals can balance their unpaid work with paid employment.
> Challenge traditional gender roles within the household so that domestic labor is equally shared.

# INTERNATIONAL TRADE

The rise of computers and the internet in the late 20th century streamlined international trade and created a global economy. This progress has driven worldwide growth and poverty reduction, but it has also faced many challenges and critics.

# Why do nations trade?

Trading between nations satisfies a need in one place with a supply from another. Countries can produce a surplus of certain products and trade these for resources or revenue.

## Benefits for all

Trading over long distances has taken place for thousands of years. For example, bronze objects from the Mediterranean were being traded with Scandinavia nearly 4,000 years ago. Economists have long argued that trade is the key to the wealth of individual nations and to higher living standards and the fairer distribution of resources around the world.

## Importing and exporting

Nations import products when they do not have the resources or capability to satisfy the demand for certain goods and services at home. Coffee, for example, is popular across Europe, but the continent does not have the right climate for growing coffee beans, so it imports from more tropical regions. Goods and services may also be imported simply because other nations are able to produce them more cheaply, in a greater volume, or to a higher standard. Most countries, for example, import electronic goods from China because its vast, skilled work force and low labor costs mean that supplies of those goods are high and their prices extremely competitive.

When a country exports goods to meet the demands of other nations, its export earnings can pay for goods and services that it needs to import. Also, where a

country produces goods over and above the demands of its own population, it may export those goods to generate further revenue for its economy. This economic weighing up of exports and imports is known as the "balance of trade" (see pp.156–157).

## American food trade

The extent of global trade is especially visible in a supermarket. Even the US, the world's richest economy, has to import 15 percent of its food, the proportions varying depending on the scale of domestic production and the level of import tariffs (see pp.166–167).

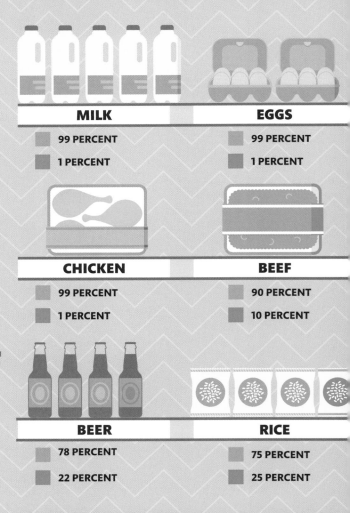

**MILK**
99 PERCENT
1 PERCENT

**EGGS**
99 PERCENT
1 PERCENT

**CHICKEN**
99 PERCENT
1 PERCENT

**BEEF**
90 PERCENT
10 PERCENT

**BEER**
78 PERCENT
22 PERCENT

**RICE**
75 PERCENT
25 PERCENT

# $**31**tn
## was the value of **world trade** in goods and services in 2022

World Trade Statistical Review (2023)

## GLOBAL TRADE GROWTH

> **The volume of world trade** was 40 times higher in 2022 than in 1950, with the value of that trade growing almost 400 times over the same period.

> **The growth in export trade** matches the growth in the global economy. Many conclude that this shows the value of trade, including American economists Jeffrey Frankel and David Romer, who presented evidence in 1999 linking increased trade with economic growth.

> **Global trade** can be adversely affected by factors beyond the control of national economies, such as fluctuating energy costs, the effects of climate change, wars, and political instability.

## ✓ NEED TO KNOW

> **Tariff** A tax imposed on goods and services imported into one country from another to raise revenue or protect domestic firms from outside competition.

> **Quota** A limit set by a government on the number or value of goods and services that a country imports or exports.

> **Free trade area** A group of countries that trade with each other free of most or all tariffs and quotas.

### WINE

- 75 PERCENT
- 25 PERCENT

### FRESH VEGETABLES

- 68 PERCENT
- 32 PERCENT

### LAMB

- 50 PERCENT
- 50 PERCENT

### FRESH FRUIT

- 45 PERCENT
- 55 PERCENT

### SPICES

- 40 PERCENT
- 60 PERCENT

### SEAFOOD

- 6 PERCENT
- 94 PERCENT

## KEY

- DOMESTIC
- IMPORTED

Approximate figures

# Balance of trade

A country's balance of trade is the difference in value between its exports and its imports. It is the significant factor in the difference between how much money flows out of a country and how much comes in.

## Surpluses and deficits

When a country exports something, it receives money from another country. When it imports something, it makes a payment. The balance of trade is the difference in value between total exports and total imports. If a country exports more than it imports, it is said to have a "trade surplus," which means it earns more than it spends. If it imports more than it exports, it has a "trade deficit," which means it spends more than it earns.

## Economic health

A country with a trade surplus is often viewed as having a healthy economy; after satisfying domestic consumers, its producers are able to earn money from other countries. However, it can also indicate a lack of demand in the domestic economy.

Similarly, a trade deficit is not necessarily a sign of weakness (see box). During a recession, a country may prefer to export more than it imports in order to boost jobs and demand in its domestic economy—but in times of expansion, it may decide to import more to increase competition. This puts a downward pressure on prices and therefore slows inflation (see pp.96–97).

## A balancing act

The simplified formula for a country's balance of trade (BOT) is the value of its exports minus the value of its imports for a given period. Exports are all outgoings, including goods and services sold, but also foreign aid and loan repayments. Imports include goods and services bought, as well as incoming aid, donations, or other payments.

# $80.6 billion
## was China's trade surplus in July 2023

www.statista.com "Monthly Balance of Trade, China" (2023)

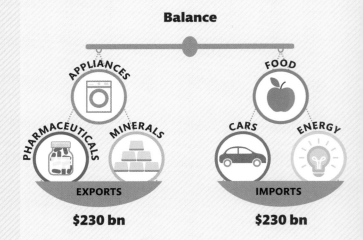

Balance

APPLIANCES
PHARMACEUTICALS
MINERALS
EXPORTS
$230 bn

FOOD
CARS
ENERGY
IMPORTS
$230 bn

**Trade balance**
When exports exactly match imports, a country is said to have balanced trade. This may seem like an ideal situation, but in practice it occurs very rarely and does not last long.

In other circumstances, persistent deficits can be problematic. A trade deficit may signal a technological lag, putting a country at a disadvantage against competitors. A significantly negative balance could also force the country to borrow more to pay for imports, or sell its assets, land, resource rights, or companies to foreign investors. If a country can neither borrow money to pay for imports nor have anything left to sell, it may need to seek the assistance of global institutions such as the International Monetary Fund (see pp.178–179).

## THE US TRADE DEFICIT

Although it has the strongest economy in the world, the US has had a trade deficit for decades. This only reversed briefly in 2008–2009, when the global financial crisis (see pp.72–73) led to a reduction in the global demand for imports. It proves that a country can enjoy a high quality of life but still run a trade deficit.

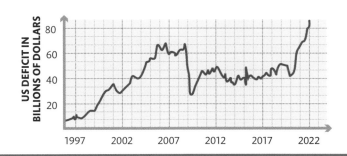

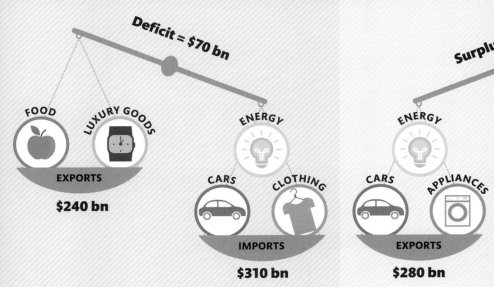

**Deficit = $70 bn**

FOOD · LUXURY GOODS

ENERGY · CARS · CLOTHING

EXPORTS
**$240 bn**

IMPORTS
**$310 bn**

### Trade deficit
When imports are more than exports, a country is said to have a negative trade balance, or a "trade deficit." This means more money is flowing out of the country than is coming in.

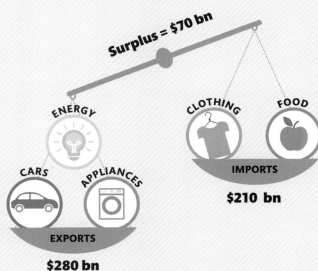

**Surplus = $70 bn**

ENERGY · CARS · APPLIANCES

CLOTHING · FOOD

EXPORTS
**$280 bn**

IMPORTS
**$210 bn**

### Trade surplus
When exports are more than imports, a country is said to have a positive trade balance, or a "trade surplus." This indicates that a country's producers have an active foreign market.

# Absolute and comparative advantage

Economists use the ideas of absolute and comparative advantage to define two different ways in which countries can trade with each other.

## Only the best

A country that has an absolute advantage over another is indisputably better placed to make a particular product, whether it has better raw materials, a cheaper or more skilled labor force, or some other advantage. Adam Smith (see pp.126–127) used this idea to explain why nations should specialize in what they do best and trade with the best producers of the other goods that they need. He argued, for example, that Britain should specialize in making cheap textiles, while Portugal, with its extensive vineyards, should specialize in making wine.

## It's all relative

British economist David Ricardo (1772–1823) developed the more nuanced idea of comparative advantage, which shows that a country does not need to have an absolute advantage to trade successfully. A country

**COUNTRY A**

**LOSER**
Country A can produce
less wine and less cheese

## Kinds of advantage

Absolute advantage is a winner-takes-all scenario that may reduce the incentive for all but the best producers to trade. However, comparative advantage shows how two nations can trade with each other, even if one has an absolute advantage in certain product areas.

**COUNTRY B**

**WINNER**
Country B can produce more
wine and more cheese

### Absolute advantage

Country B can produce twice as much wine and 50 percent more cheese for the same cost as country A. It has an absolute advantage in exporting to country A.

has a comparative advantage if it can make a product at a lower opportunity cost (see pp.22–23) than its competitors—in other words, in some way more efficiently (see below). Ricardo also noted that if all countries specialize in goods for which they have a comparative advantage, then both producers and consumers benefit from lower production costs and lower retail prices. However, as Ricardo's critics pointed out, a country can specialize too much: if it depends entirely on another country for food, it may starve if trade is disrupted.

> "A country may ... import corn even if it can be grown [at home] with less labour ..."

David Ricardo, *On the Principles of Political Economy and Taxation* (1817)

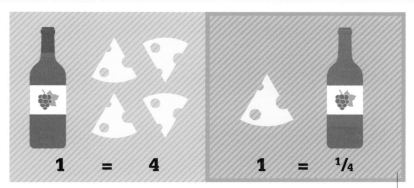

**1 = 4**

**COUNTRY A**

**WINNER**
It costs country A comparatively less to make cheese than wine

**1 = 1/4**

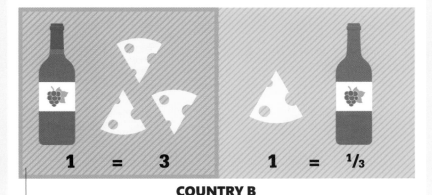

**1 = 3**

**COUNTRY B**

**LOSER**
It costs country B comparatively more to make cheese than wine

**1 = 1/3**

## CASE STUDY

### The US and Mexico

In 2023, Mexico became the leading trading partner of the US. One reason for this is that Mexico has labor-intensive, foreign-owned vehicle-assembly plants that can assemble vehicles more efficiently for export than the US. As a result of this comparative advantage—which is based on cheap labor—the Mexican factories build vehicles out of parts that are imported from the US.

### Comparative advantage

In country A, one cheese costs ¼ bottle of wine to make, but in country B, it costs $1/3$ of a bottle. This means that country A has a comparative advantage in making cheese.

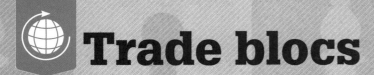

# Trade blocs

**Countries are increasingly coming together to form trade blocs, which enable them to trade more freely with each other but less so with the rest of the world.**

## Economic bonds

When a country trades with other countries, it can do so either bilaterally (by making an agreement with one other country at a time) or multilaterally (by making an agreement with several countries simultaneously). Countries that are bound by multilateral agreements are known as "trade blocs," and today, hardly a country in the world is not a member of at least one bloc or another. Trade blocs ensure that customs and other trade tariffs are reduced between members, who therefore pay lower prices for imported goods and therefore can increase their exports, achieve economies of scale, and enjoy higher growth. The downside to trade blocs is that they effectively price nonmember countries out of their markets. However, those countries usually form trade blocs of their own.

Some trade blocs begin as agreements intended to ensure that formerly warring countries remain at peace. The European Union (EU), for example, grew out of an agreement made in 1951 that was designed to integrate Europe's coal and steel industries—particularly those of France and Germany, which were enemies during World War II (1939–1945)—but rapidly grew into the European Economic Community. At the same time, the US established the General Agreement on Tariffs and Trade (GATT), which was devoted to restoring world trade in the postwar period. GATT was initially signed by 23 countries, but it was replaced in 1995 by the World Trade Organization (WTO), which facilitates trade between over 160 countries.

## Strained ties

As the recent history of the EU shows, tensions can develop between member states of trade blocs, particularly when some feel that others have begun to wield undue amounts of power. This was one reason why the UK left the EU in 2020, despite the potential damage to its economy.

## Economic alliances

Trade blocs are intergovernmental agreements that enable member countries to trade more efficiently with each other. Today, the biggest trade blocs in the world are the USMCA, the EU, the AFCFTA, the CPTPP, Mercosur, and the RCEP.

### USMCA

The United States-Mexico-Canada Agreement (2020) is the dominant trade bloc of North America. Successor to the North American Free Trade Agreement (NAFTA), it includes the US, Canada, and Mexico and creates 17 percent of global GDP.

### EU

The European Union (1992) has 27 members and, as of 2022, a combined GDP of $16 trillion, making it the world's third-largest economy. Although not members, Iceland, Liechtenstein, Norway, and Switzerland also have access to the EU.

## CPTPP

The Comprehensive and Progressive agreement for Trans-Pacific Partnership (2018) covers Japan, Malaysia, Vietnam, Australia, Singapore, Brunei, New Zealand, Canada, Mexico, Peru, Chile, and the UK.

## RCEP

The Regional Comprehensive Economic Partnership (2022) is the world's biggest trading bloc in terms of GDP. China, Australia, Japan, Malaysia, and New Zealand are among its 15 member states.

## AFCFTA

One of the newest trading blocs, the African Continental Free Trade Area (2020) includes 55 countries, totaling 1.3 billion people, and aims to eliminate over half of the trade tariffs between them.

## MERCOSUR

The Southern Common Market (1991) was set up by Argentina, Brazil, Paraguay, and Uruguay. Suriname, Guyana, Colombia, Ecuador, Peru, Chile, and Bolivia all have associate status. In 2021, Mercosur was the world's fifth-largest economy.

## TYPES OF TRADE BLOCS

❯ **Preferential trade area** An area that charges lower tariffs for certain goods and services.

❯ **Free trade area** A region composed of countries that have signed a free trade agreement, which enables those countries to trade cheaply with each other.

❯ **Customs union** A free trade area in which member countries charge external countries the same customs tariffs.

❯ **Single market** Also known as a common market, a bloc that has no trade barriers and enables freedom of movement for goods, capital, services, and labor.

❯ **Economic and monetary union** A bloc that has a common market, a customs union, and the same currency.

"Europe will be forged in crises, and will be the sum of the solutions adopted for those crises."

Jean Monnet, a founding father of the EU, *Mémoires* (1976)

# Free trade

Free trade agreements enable countries to buy and sell goods across borders with few restrictions. Economists champion free trade because it promotes competition on an international scale.

## The case for free trade

Governments often find it politically popular to impose barriers on imports to protect domestic firms and jobs (see pp.166–167). However, economists have long argued that protectionism stifles trade and is ultimately damaging to everyone involved. They promote free trade because it encourages growth and enables countries to specialize in what they do best (see pp.158–159). Free trade increases competition,

making goods and services cheaper. By contrast, barriers—such as tariffs, quotas, and unfair practices like subsidies—reduce competition, which increases costs and doesn't encourage firms to be efficient.

In the 19th century, many British economists promoted free trade as the country's colonial empire expanded rapidly. After World War II (1939–1945), increased economic cooperation saw nations reduce barriers with initiatives like

the General Agreement on Tariffs and Trade (see pp. 178–179). Many joined together in formal trading blocs, such as the European Union (see pp.160–161). Members of these groups can trade freely, albeit with regulations and oversight.

## Free trade problems

Some economists criticize free trade because industrial jobs in developed countries have declined in the face of competition from

## Trading partners

For the last four centuries, economists have primarily focused on strategies to make their country the wealthiest. "Mercantilists" thought the key was to pile up their country's gold reserves. "Free traders" believed in maximizing trade for all nations.

**IMPORT GOODS WITH TARIFFS**

**EXPORT GOODS AT HIGH PRICES**

**Country A**

**Country B**

### Mercantilism
Mercantilism dominated economics from the 16th to 18th centuries. Mercantilists thought the best way to build a nation's wealth was to increase exports and restrict imports, thereby bringing increasingly more gold into the country.

cheaper labor abroad. They argue that "sunrise" (new) industries need protection from the competition of free trade, and "sunset" (declining) industries need space to recover and rebuild (see p.169).

Other economists believe the whole idea of free trade needs to be rethought because it has simply become a means for rich countries to get richer, and the gap between the richest and the poorest has increased. They argue that poorer countries need to protect their economies while they develop them to the point where they are able to compete on a level playing field with richer countries.

## PROS AND CONS OF FREE TRADE

### Pros

Economists have long been advocates of free trade because it boosts economic activity.

❯ **Lower prices and better-quality goods** Consumers benefit from increased competition.

❯ **Specialization** If a nation does not have to make everything, it can focus on what it does best.

❯ **Increased demand** Domestic producers benefit from consumers having extra cash to spend.

❯ **Extra jobs** New export industries can create employment.

### Cons

The supercharged competition that free trade encourages has many casualties.

❯ **Reduced standards** Social and environmental rights protections may be lost as barriers between countries disappear.

❯ **Failing firms** Domestic firms can lose out to foreign ones, especially when they are new or old.

❯ **Lower wages** Domestic firms may have to cut wages to compete.

❯ **Job losses** As domestic firms close, unemployment rises.

"A country serves its own interests by pursuing free trade regardless of what other countries may do."

Paul Krugman, American economist, "What should trade negotiators negotiate about?," *Journal of Economic Literature*, Vol. 35, No. 1 (1997)

**IMPORT GOODS WITHOUT RESTRICTIONS**

**EXPORT GOODS WITHOUT RESTRICTIONS**

Country A

Country B

**Free trade**
Free trade challenged the idea of mercantilism. Its advocates argued that removing all barriers to trade enables everyone to benefit from the resulting growth in economic activity.

# Gravity models

Taking its cue from its counterpart in physics, the gravity theory in economics states that the larger economies are (based on their GDPs), the more trade they will do with each other.

## The gravity equation

In 1962, Dutch economist Jan Tinbergen (1903–1994) proposed that the flow of trade between countries might be predicted by what he called a "gravity equation." British physicist Isaac Newton (1642–1726) had shown that the gravitational attraction between planets is inversely proportional to their mass and the distance between them. Tinbergen argued that the bigger two economies are and the closer they are geographically, the more trade they will do with each other. In other words, countries trade most with their largest neighbors and with far-flung giants instead of with smaller local countries.

## From hypothesis to theory

At first, Tinbergen's hypothesis was just that—an ingenious intuition concerning the nature of trade that had little evidence to support it. In fact, it went

## The power of attraction

One reason for the gravity model's success has been its flexibility. The core of the theory is that attraction between economies is based on the size of GDP and physical proximity. However, similarity in politics, culture, language, and technology, and many other variables, may also play a part. The closer countries are in all respects, the more they trade (see pp.160–161).

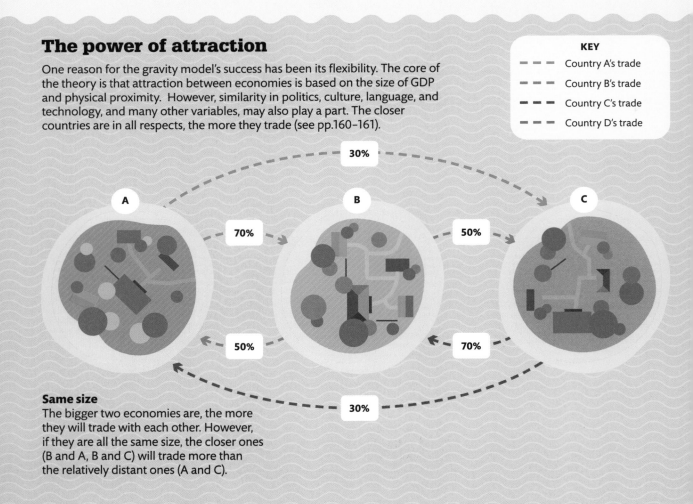

**KEY**
- - - Country A's trade
- - - Country B's trade
- - - Country C's trade
- - - Country D's trade

A · B · C

30%

70%   50%

50%   70%

30%

**Same size**
The bigger two economies are, the more they will trade with each other. However, if they are all the same size, the closer ones (B and A, B and C) will trade more than the relatively distant ones (A and C).

against most of the established ideas about what drives international trade, such as the theories of absolute and comparative advantage (see pp.158–159). However, the gravity equation proved to be so successful in predicting trade patterns that many economists were persuaded to try to incorporate it into their trade theories. Nevertheless, some economists maintain that the gravity model will soon be made redundant as developments in global transportation and communications make location irrelevant to the question of which countries should trade with each other.

## NEIGHBORS

### *The US and Canada*

Canada and the US are not just neighbors with a shared border 5,525 miles (8,891 km) long—they also have one of the biggest bilateral trade flows of any two countries in the world. In 2022, the trade between them was worth $1.2 trillion dollars. Trade with the US is more than two-thirds of Canada's entire global trade. This close and huge trading partnership depends on shared geography, similar values, common interests, strong cultural connections, and powerful economic ties.

# "The dominant role [is] played by ... exporters' and importers' GNP and distance."

Jan Tinbergen, *Shaping the World Economy: Suggestions for an International Economic Policy* (1962)

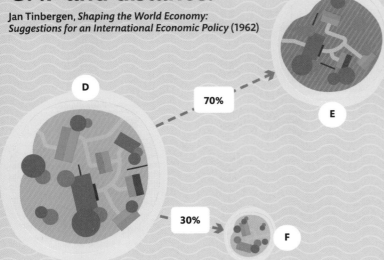

**D**

**70%**

**E**

**30%**

**F**

**Different sizes**
Nearby countries share more trade than distant countries. However, country D may trade more with a large distant country (E) than a smaller local one (F).

## OTHER FACTORS

**Historical links**
Shared history, such as the colonial ties between the UK and the Commonwealth, foster extra trade.

**Shared language**
Linguistic and cultural similarities strengthen trade by making communication even about basics such as specifications and quantities much easier.

**Time zones**
Being in similar time zones makes doing business easier. Far less trading can be done if work times are different.

**Market preferences**
Countries with similar levels of education and technology tend to be in the market for similar goods and services.

# Trade restrictions

Governments often impose restrictions on international trade either to protect their own producers or for broader political reasons. Known as "protectionism," these restrictions include sanctions, quotas, and import tariffs.

## Home protection

Most governments are aware that unchecked foreign competition can be economically damaging. Having cheaper or better-quality imports may benefit consumers, but it can also lead to job losses and wage cuts that can devastate the domestic economy. To avoid this scenario, governments impose trade barriers on foreign goods and services to tip the balance in favor of domestic producers. A government might, for instance, impose a tariff (see pp.168–169) on imported sugar. This would mean that domestically produced sugar would become comparatively cheaper, which would encourage consumers to buy it and keep money in the pockets of domestic producers.

One of the drawbacks of imposing tariffs is that, with less competition, home producers may become less efficient and less innovative. Barriers can also hurt consumers who rely on imported products and domestic producers who require imported components. Trade wars may break out if a tariffed country retaliates with restrictions of its own.

## Border controls

Protectionist policies can take many forms and often have a political instead of a purely economic purpose. In 2018, under his "America First" agenda, President Donald Trump imposed a 20 percent tariff on the first 1.2 million washing machines imported into the US, which rose to 50 percent the following year.

### Tariffs

Taxes added to imported goods to protect domestic suppliers from foreign competition are called tariffs (see pp.168–169).

### Quotas

Limits on how much of a product can be imported from another country are known as quotas. For example, China has a quota on imports of Cambodian rice.

### Nontariff barriers

Also known as Technical Barriers to Trade, nontariff barriers are regulations—often concerning safety—that make it hard for imports to sell in a domestic market.

## Sanctions

In extreme circumstances, governments may impose sanctions on another country as a way of projecting political power. These sanctions can take many forms, from travel bans to trade embargoes and asset seizures. They can be powerful policy tools, but they can also be hard to apply—and they can hurt the sanctioning country if it relies on the other's exports. Their effectiveness is also not guaranteed. Sanctions against apartheid-era South Africa are often credited with helping end apartheid in the early 1990s. However, when Russia invaded Ukraine in 2022, the EU and the US imposed the widest range of sanctions ever seen, with debatable effectiveness.

## DUMPING

Some countries engage in a practice known as "dumping," whereby they flood foreign markets with products that they sell at prices that are lower than they are in their domestic markets. By doing so, they undercut local producers, who cannot sell their products. Many countries impose tariffs or quotas (see below) on specific imports to prevent this from happening.

COUNTRY A          COUNTRY B

# "Historically, free trade is the exception and protectionism the rule."

Paul Bairoch, Swiss economic historian, *Economics and World History: Myths and Paradoxes* (1993)

## Voluntary export restraints (VERs)

Agreements between countries to limit specific imports are called VERs. In the 1980s, the US government used VERs to slow imports of Japanese cars to 1.68 million a year.

## Subsidies

A subsidy is a financial aid from governments to give local producers an advantage. For example, in 1962, the EU introduced its Common Agricultural Policy to subsidize European farmers.

## Embargoes

An embargo is a government order to stop trade with particular countries. The US imposed a trade embargo on Cuba after Fidel Castro came to power.

## Additional barriers

Governments use their ingenuity to target particular imports. For example, they often charge a percentage of a good's value—such as the 15 percent tax that Japan levies on American cars. Other goods may only be available to businesses that buy licenses to import them.

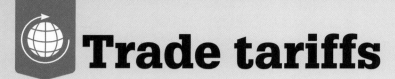

# Trade tariffs

**A common method that countries use to protect their industries from foreign competition is to apply trade tariffs to imported goods and services.**

## Limiting imports

All governments implement some form of protective policy for their domestic firms, workers, and consumers (see pp.166–167). Their intention is to protect jobs for their citizens; support small firms and industries; raise revenues; and provide national security through self-sufficiency in food, energy, and defense. These protectionist policies typically focus on imports, adding tariffs (taxes) onto foreign goods and services in order to ensure that domestic equivalents remain preferable to consumers. This sustains domestic firms and maintains employment and wage rates.

Tariffs may also be applied due to quality and safety concerns. Many countries have different regulatory standards in areas such as food preparation and intellectual property protection, so a country may restrict imports that do not meet its own domestic standards.

## Political tools

Tariffs bring revenue into a country, so they reduce the tax burden on citizens—a fact that pro-tariff policymakers may stress. They can also strengthen or weaken a country's bonds with other countries—for example, by applying a tariff to all steel imports except those from a select group of trading partners or allies. Tariffs therefore play a key role in international politics, where they can be used as bargaining chips during negotiations between countries. Trade blocs, such as the European Union and Mercosur (see pp.160–161), are groups of countries that have had such negotiations and have agreed to trade freely with each other while continuing to charge tariffs to nonmember countries.

Although most countries today belong to a trade bloc, each nation has to strike its own balance between protecting its own industries and importing what it needs from abroad.

## Types of tariffs

Import tariffs may be applied to all imports, or they may target specific products. This may be done in different ways—by weight or number, as a percentage of their market value, or as a combination of the two. Today, high tariffs tend to be charged by developing countries, partly as a way of increasing government revenues. Developed countries, being less reliant on income, generally favor nontariff trade barriers (see pp.166–167).

**Exporter**

# "Tariff policy victims are mostly invisible."

Walter E. Williams, American economist, *Liberty Versus the Tyranny of Socialism: Controversial Essays* (2013)

## PROTECTING INDUSTRIES

One argument for trade tariffs is that they protect domestic firms in both "sunrise" (emerging) and "sunset" (declining) sectors. Sunrise industries need protecting until they are established, whereas sunset industries need protecting until new domestic firms can replace them. Without help, sunset industries will not be able to compete if foreign equivalents offer better value for money.

**Importer**

### Specific tariffs

A specific tariff is a tax imposed on specific types of imported goods and does not depend on the value of those goods. It is usually based on the weight or number of the goods—for example, $1 per pound, or per 100 units, of a specific product.

### Other tariffs

An ad valorem tariff (from the Latin term for "according to value") is a percentage of what a product is worth; combined with a specific tax, it becomes a "compound tariff." A tariff-rate quota is tax that increases when the quantity of a product rises above a specified threshold.

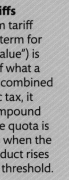

**Importer**

# Development economics

Instead of focusing only on boosting economic activity in developing nations, development economics also aims to improve the quality of life and opportunity in local communities.

## An integrated approach

Proponents of development economics, such as Indian economist Amartya Sen (b. 1933) and American economist Jeffrey D. Sachs (b. 1954), argue that it is not enough to focus purely on the goal of economic growth (see pp.90–91). It is also necessary, they say, to address the factors that improve people's well-being, including quality of life, education, and health care. These issues are not simply humanitarian concerns, but must be part of a complete strategy for economic development.

## Overcoming hurdles

Development economists have created theoretical models to show routes to economic and social prosperity, including social improvements and technical innovation, as well as fiscal policy—the use of government spending and taxation to influence the economy (see pp.110–111). In particular, they help developing countries identify and overcome their obstacles to growth, such as poverty, inequality (see pp.122–123), and market failure (see pp.36–37).

When it comes to India, Amartya Sen highlights that, despite massive economic growth and the country's rise to become a major player in global markets, it is still wracked by hunger and poor investment in basic needs, such as health and education. He argues that without tackling these issues, economic growth is neither sustainable nor ethical (see pp.142–143).

## PROVIDING BASIC SUSTENANCE

❯ **Enough food** is an absolute essential for sustaining life and health.

❯ **Reliable shelter** is equally important.

❯ **Quality health care** is critical for maintaining a community's health, reducing child mortality, and raising life expectancy overall.

❯ **Safety and security** are vital—safety for individuals in their communities and national security for the state.

## Defining development

Michael Todaro (b. 1942), an American pioneer of development economics, identified the three core aims for development shown here. Todaro sees development not simply as a target for economic growth, but also as a multidimensional process to transform a community's entire economic and social system.

> **"Poverty is not just a lack of money; it is not having the capability to realize one's full potential as a human being."**

Amartya Sen, *Development as Freedom* (1999)

## ENRICHING LIFE AND BUILDING SELF-ESTEEM

❯ **A higher standard of living** includes higher incomes and more jobs.

❯ **Good education** strengthens cultural and human values, leading to greater individual and national self-esteem.

❯ **Established social, political, and economic** systems and institutions can promote dignity and self-respect.

## INCREASING FREEDOM OF CHOICE

❯ **Liberated people** are free from servitude, dependence on others, and ignorance.

❯ **Empowered people** have the ability to make their own economic and social choices.

❯ **Genuine choice** allows people to satisfy their wants.

## HISTORICAL APPROACHES

Over the centuries, countries have had different perspectives on how to develop their economies, each reflecting their cultural values of the time.

### Mercantilism

From the 16th to the 18th centuries, European nations used trade surpluses and bans on silver and gold exports to limit exposure to rivals.

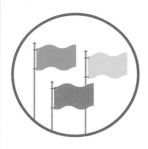

### Economic nationalism

In the 19th century, rich nations opposed free trade (see pp.162–163) and protected their economy through tariffs and other barriers (see pp.166–169).

### Structural change

This theory was directed at the complete shift of a nation's economic focus, such as the USSR's rapid industrialization in the 1920s and 1930s.

### Linear growth

Inspired by the 1948 Marshall Plan for Europe's recovery after World War II, the linear growth model saw industrialization as the necessary starting point for further growth.

# Trade and development

**Three-quarters of the world's countries have "developing economies"—in other words, have relatively low standards of living, income, and economic and industrial development.**

## The wealth gap

Income, wealth, and consumption are distributed unevenly across the world, leading to inequality (see pp.122–123). For example, the World Bank reports that Burundi had an average income of $238 per person in 2022, compared to $126,426 for Luxembourg and $76,398 for the US. Poorer countries are sometimes classified as "developing," though definitions for this vary, and some people argue that the term is misleading, outdated, and overly simplistic.

The International Monetary Fund (IMF, see p.113) identifies three key features of "developing and emerging" economies: a low average income per person, a low diversity of exports, and low participation in the financial system. It classifies 152 countries as having developing and emerging economies. They are home to more than 85 percent of the world's population and include all countries

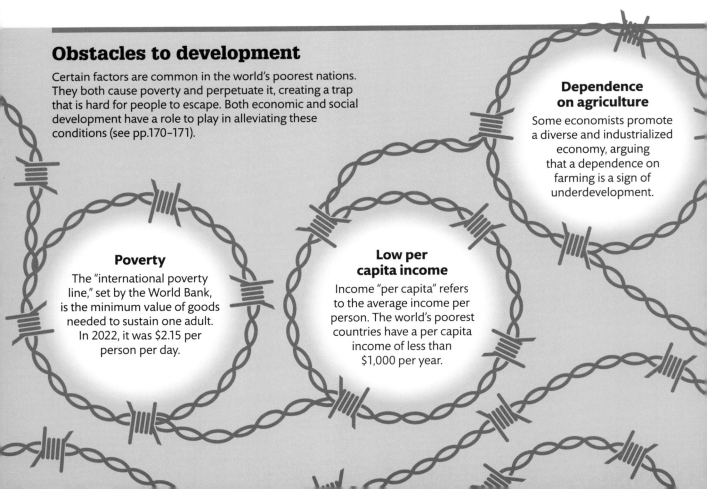

## Obstacles to development

Certain factors are common in the world's poorest nations. They both cause poverty and perpetuate it, creating a trap that is hard for people to escape. Both economic and social development have a role to play in alleviating these conditions (see pp.170–171).

**Dependence on agriculture**
Some economists promote a diverse and industrialized economy, arguing that a dependence on farming is a sign of underdevelopment.

**Poverty**
The "international poverty line," set by the World Bank, is the minimum value of goods needed to sustain one adult. In 2022, it was $2.15 per person per day.

**Low per capita income**
Income "per capita" refers to the average income per person. The world's poorest countries have a per capita income of less than $1,000 per year.

in Africa and Central and South America, most in Asia, and many island states.

## Is trade the solution?

Many economists argue that trade and globalization (the worldwide interaction of economies) are raising standards of living. They point to the transformation of Asia–Pacific economies, such as South Korea. Others suggest that globalization is increasing the divide between rich and poor. In 2023, Oxfam reported that during the previous decade, the richest 1 percent had captured half of all new wealth.

## ECONOMIC GROWTH AND EXPORTS

Gross domestic product (GDP) measures economic activity (see pp.88–89). As a share of global GDP, exports have accelerated over the last 150 years, which some economists suggest is proof that trade boosts development.

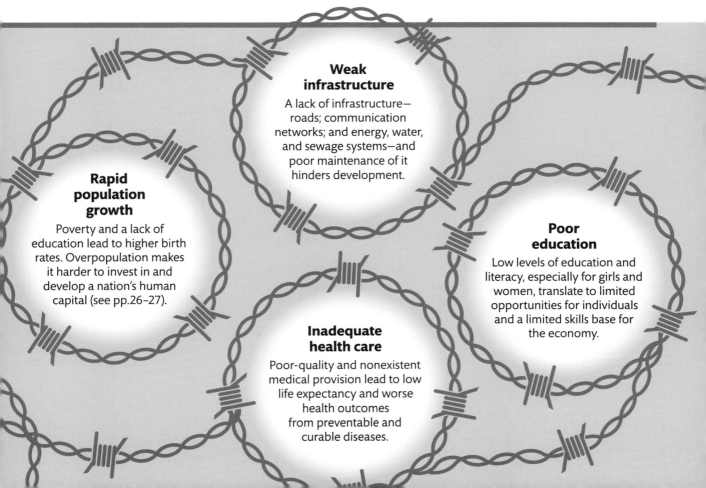

**Weak infrastructure**
A lack of infrastructure—roads; communication networks; and energy, water, and sewage systems—and poor maintenance of it hinders development.

**Rapid population growth**
Poverty and a lack of education lead to higher birth rates. Overpopulation makes it harder to invest in and develop a nation's human capital (see pp.26–27).

**Poor education**
Low levels of education and literacy, especially for girls and women, translate to limited opportunities for individuals and a limited skills base for the economy.

**Inadequate health care**
Poor-quality and nonexistent medical provision lead to low life expectancy and worse health outcomes from preventable and curable diseases.

# Ethical trade

The ethical trade and Fairtrade movements strive to ensure that the workers making the goods and services we buy do their work in good, safe conditions and are being paid properly for their labor.

### The birth of an idea

In the 13th century, Italian philosopher and theologian Thomas Aquinas (1225–1274) talked about the idea of a "just price." A dealer, he asserted, may charge a price that includes a decent profit, but excessive profiteering is sinful. He proposed that a "just" price is the price the buyer freely agrees to pay. Modern market economists, however, insist that there is no moral dimension to pricing—that it is simply an automatic response to the balance between supply and demand in a free market. But people across the world are challenging this view, compelling economists and governments to consider ethics.

### Ethical and fair

The ethical trade movement originated in the 1990s, when campaigns and media exposés highlighted harsh conditions for workers producing items such

## The coffee crisis

The Fairtrade movement grew out of an awareness that producers were not being paid fairly for coffee and bananas. In 2002, an Oxfam report—"Mugged: Poverty in your coffee cup"—traced prices paid for a kilogram of coffee grown in Uganda through the supply chain, showing how profit margins suddenly widen when the coffee reaches the roasters and retailers.

| Farmer | Buyer | Exporter | International dealer |
|---|---|---|---|
| 14¢ | 26¢ | 45¢ | $1.64 |
| The farmer may work all year to grow coffee, but is paid just 14¢ for a kilogram (kg) of coffee beans. | The buyer sells the beans to an exporter for 26¢ per kg. This includes 5¢ for the buyer, plus transport and other costs. | The exporter grades and packages the beans, then sells them to international dealers for 45¢ per kg. | The dealer sells on to big multinational roasters at $1.64 per kg—many times more than the price the farmer receives. |

as clothes, shoes, toys, and food for multinational companies. It drove retailers and big-name brands to improve conditions for workers throughout their supply chains and to respect environmental standards.

The initiative complements the Fairtrade movement, founded in the 1980s, which helps secure fair terms of trade and prices for vulnerable suppliers in the developing world. Whereas ethical trade concentrates on the behavior of buying companies, ensuring they meet labor standards and codes of practice, Fairtrade focuses on getting suppliers a better deal and workers better conditions. A Fairtrade Mark label on a product shows that it meets the internationally agreed social, environmental, and economic Fairtrade Standards.

 **CASE STUDY**

### Tragedy in Bangladesh

On April 24, 2013, the Rana Plaza clothing factory on the outskirts of Dhaka in Bangladesh suddenly collapsed, killing 1,134 people and injuring thousands more. The clothing found among the ruins carried the labels of many major Western brands, from Prada and Versace to Primark and Walmart. The tragedy played a huge part in alerting the world to the horrors of the fashion industry, in which workers make clothes in appalling and unsafe conditions for very low wages.

# 1,880 is the number of producer organizations certified by Fairtrade in 71 countries

www.fairtrade.org.uk, 2023

$10

#### Roaster
The roaster, who turns the beans into instant coffee granules, inflates the price even more.

$26.40

#### Retailer
The instant coffee granules are sold in Western supermarkets at a price of $26.40 per kg.

**14¢ PER KG OF UNPROCESSED BEANS**

↓

**$26.40 PER KG OF INSTANT COFFEE**

=

#### 7,000% INCREASE
Taking into account that 2.6 kg of original beans are needed to make 1 kg of instant coffee.

#### An enormous leap
From bean to cup, the price of coffee increases hugely—by 7,000%.

# The foreign sector

In every economy, money flows in circles between consumers and producers both domestically and in what economists call the "foreign sector."

## The fourth sector

A nation's economy is divided into three domestic sectors—households, the government, and businesses (including financial institutions)—and a foreign sector, which concerns trade with the rest of the world. Foreign trade is of two main kinds: imports and exports of goods and services (see pp.156–157) and capital flows (the inward and outward flow of financial assets, such as equities and bonds; see pp.188–189).

The foreign sector extends the circular flow of money between domestic producers and consumers (see pp.84–85) to include all transactions beyond a country's borders. Of the domestic sectors, government and businesses both export and import to and from other countries, while households just buy imports traded from abroad.

## Imports and exports

Economists often combine imports and exports in the concept of "net exports." This describes the amount of money a country makes from exports after its imports have been deducted. Positive net exports are when exports exceed imports; negative net exports are when imports exceed exports. If exports exceed imports, then the circular flow of money through all sectors of the economy increases. If imports exceed exports, the overall flow slows as the economy is deprived of money.

Imports are seen as a "leakage" from the economy because they represent money lost from the circular flow (see p.84). Exports, on the other hand, are viewed as an economic "injection" because they add to the circular flow and provide more money for producers to invest in goods and services. Leakages and injections can have direct effects on an economy, such as falls or rises in national income, unemployment, and spending.

## CLOSED ECONOMY

A closed economy is one that does not trade or exchange money with any other, but in today's globalized world, such self-sufficiency is almost impossible. By comparing a country's imports and exports to its GDP (see pp.88–89), economists can measure how closed an economy is. Currently, Brazil's economy is the nearest to being closed; as a portion of its GDP, it imports the least amount of goods in the world.

DOMESTIC ECONOMY

NO EXPORTS

NO IMPORTS

NO FOREIGN AID

OTHER COUNTRIES

## In and out

Money enters the economy as the government and businesses sell goods and services to other countries and pay wages to the people who provide them (the household sector). Money leaves when the country imports foreign goods and services. The economy is also fueled by taxes raised by the government and spent on public services.

FOREIGN SECTOR

PAYMENT FOR EXPORTS

PAYMENT FOR IMPORTS

PAYMENT FOR EXPORTS

PAYMENT FOR IMPORTS

"For the only way ... a durable peace can be created is [through] international trade."

James Forrestal, US Secretary of Defense, memorandum (1947)

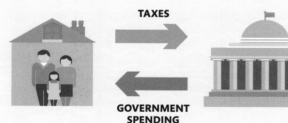

TAXES

TAXES

GOVERNMENT SPENDING

GOVERNMENT SPENDING

**Household sector**
Households engage in the economy by working and spending money on goods and services. Many of the services households pay for are provided by the government.

**Government sector**
The government receives taxes from households and businesses. It uses the money to pay for public services such as health care.

**Business sector**
Firms receive money from households and the government for selling products and services. In return, they pay wages and taxes.

# Global trade organizations

To facilitate international trade, governments have come together to form a range of global trade organizations. They set common rules for trading and provide forums for discussion and settling disputes.

## A world forum

The idea of creating organizations for global trade emerged after World War II (1939–1945). This new era of international economic cooperation grew out of a desire to avoid more conflict and prevent a repetition of the economic and political troubles that had followed World War I (1914–1918). In 1947, 23 countries set up the General Agreement on Tariffs and Trade (GATT). Its mission was to promote international trade by reducing or eliminating barriers, such as tariffs or quotas (see pp.166–167). By 1986, GATT had nearly 150 members.

## Building on success

In 1995, GATT was superseded by the World Trade Organization (WTO). It creates and enforces rules that provide confidence and stability in the global marketplace, lower trade barriers, and increase the bonds between nations.

The rules of the WTO are multilateral—they are made by all member states and ratified in every home parliament. Countries sign agreements that are effectively contracts guaranteeing trading rights. Examples of other WTO

## Global cooperation

International trade organizations like the WTO aim to increase the living standards of all their members through improved trade, although special attention is given to assist developing countries. The organizations also address cross-border issues, such as climate change; sustainable development; and global challenges, such as the COVID-19 pandemic.

### Goods

The WTO works to lower barriers to the trade of goods. It also deals with product standards, unfair subsidies, and dumping—where one country sells goods in another at prices that undercut those in the local economy (see pp.166–167).

# 98%
## of world trade is carried out by the members of the WTO
World Trade Organization (2023)

### Services

The General Agreement on Trade in Services (GATS) provides service industries—for example, banking, hotels, and transportation—with the same support and protections that producers of goods get.

initiatives include the liberalization of telecommunications, tariff-free trade in information technology products, and the provision of affordable medicine for poorer economies. In 2023, the WTO also joined with the European Union (EU) to create a program for boosting foreign investment in the world's poorer countries.

## OTHER GLOBAL ORGANIZATIONS

❯ **The Organization for Economic Co-operation and Development** (OECD) promotes cooperation among advanced market economies to boost their trade.

❯ **The World Customs Organization** (WCO) works on customs-related matters, from rules of origin to illegal drugs and weapons trading.

❯ **The United Nations Conference on Trade and Development** (UNCTAD) promotes the interests of developing countries.

❯ **The United Nation Food and Agriculture Organization** (FAO) leads international efforts to achieve food security for all.

### Intellectual property

Trade-Related Aspects of Intellectual Property Rights (TRIPS) outlines how members must protect copyrights, patents, trademarks, inventions, industrial designs, and trade secrets.

### The World Trade Organization

By 2023, the WTO had 164 members, which represents over 80 percent of all nations. The organization aims to encourage the free flow of trade around the world, settle disputes, and negotiate trade rules and agreements based particularly on its five main areas of activity.

### Dispute settlement

The Dispute Settlement Understanding (DSU) helps governments resolve trade conflicts through discussion and, if necessary, consultation with a panel of experts.

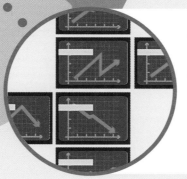

### Trade monitoring

Monitoring how members are implementing agreements is central to the WTO's work. Every six months, it issues its own reports, as well as joint reports with the OECD and UNCTAD (see box, above).

# FINANCE

The management of money is known as finance. It guides decisions about how people should raise, spend, and invest money. Finance can include managing debt, risk analysis, and understanding how different financial markets work.

# Money

For economists, money is anything that could be exchanged for goods or services—not just bills and coins. It serves as a store of value and as a medium of exchange.

## Why do we have money?

People could do away with money and simply exchange goods of roughly equal value using a barter system. But this relies on both sides having something the other wants—a challenge known as the "double coincidence of wants," which takes time and effort to overcome.

Money, on the other hand, makes trading far more efficient. Where money is involved, there will always be willing traders because funds received from one exchange can be used freely and widely for other exchanges. This describes the main purpose of money, as a medium of exchange—something that is widely accepted in return for goods or services. Money also acts as a unit of account: because everything is priced using a common unit, it is easy to compare the value of things. Money is a store of value, too—a way of preserving wealth for future use. If earnings were paid in cheese, they would need to be eaten before they went bad, whereas money will keep. These uses for money indicate the properties it must have: it must be durable in order to store value; it must be commonly accepted to act as a medium of exchange and a unit of account; and it must be easily divisible to be convenient to use.

### MEASURING MONEY

There are various measures of the amount of money in the economy at any time. They differ in terms of what they include, besides currency (notes and coins), as money. Some measures also include, among other things, bank deposits that cannot be accessed on demand. The two best known are the money supply and the monetary base.

> **The money supply** is the most common measure. It includes all currency in circulation, plus demand deposits (accessed on demand) held in banks.

> **The monetary base** includes all currency in circulation, plus reserves held at the central bank. It is also known as "high-powered money," because its increase can lead to a much larger increase in the overall money supply (a ratio dubbed the "money multiplier").

## The evolution of money

Over the centuries, money has appeared in many forms. People moved from barter systems to using objects as mediums of exchange. This led to the development of coins and then to paper money that was linked to commodities. "Fiat money," which is not linked to commodities and has no underlying value, is the dominant form of money today. Whatever form money takes, it provides a standard value against which any item can be compared.

### c. 6000 BCE

**1. Exchange of objects**

People in early societies traded items of a similar value using a barter system. For example, a farmer could exchange a bushel of wheat for part of a butchered sheep. An inefficient system, it took effort to find a fair trade.

*7th century CE*

*20th century*

**5. Credit and debit cards**

Credit cards (introduced in 1958) and debit cards (1982) allow for the easy transfer of money between bank accounts. Most money now exists electronically as part of people's bank balances instead of as physical currency.

## 2. Commodity money

Over time, easily traded and stored goods—such as gold or animal skins—functioned as money. The Ancient Egyptians are thought to have been the first people to use gold for exchanging and bartering.

c. 3000 BCE

## 4. Paper money

First used in China in the 7th century, paper money was commodity money that could be exchanged for its stated value of coins. Nowadays, paper money is "fiat money"—legal tender with no intrinsic value.

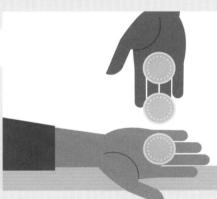

## 3. Coins

Preweighed, certified pieces of precious metal, coins were durable, divisible, and easy to use. The earliest known coin-production facility (mint)—found in Henan Province, China, in 2021—dates back to 640 BCE.

640 BCE

2009

## 6. Cryptocurrency

Cryptocurrency, such as Bitcoin, is not linked to a commodity or issued by a government or central bank. Instead, people transfer and exchange digital tokens directly with each other (see pp.214–215).

# Borrowing and saving

People borrow or save money to keep their consumption levels relatively stable. However, both borrowing and saving are influenced by interest rates, which can favor either one or the other over time.

## Planning ahead

Instead of having a feast today and a famine tomorrow, most people prefer to consume a moderate amount on both days. However, if someone expects their income to rise in the future, they may decide to borrow to start consuming some of that extra income—even though repaying the money will reduce future consumption. This increase in current consumption and decrease in future consumption stabilizes the person's consumption over time. Similarly, if someone

expects their income to fall in the future—such as when they retire—they may decide to save in the present. They may also save as protection against a future hazard, such as becoming unemployed.

## Changing interest rates

A key factor in whether people decide to borrow or save is the interest rate. If the interest rate on loans increases, then loans become more expensive and borrowers borrow less—which means that they reduce

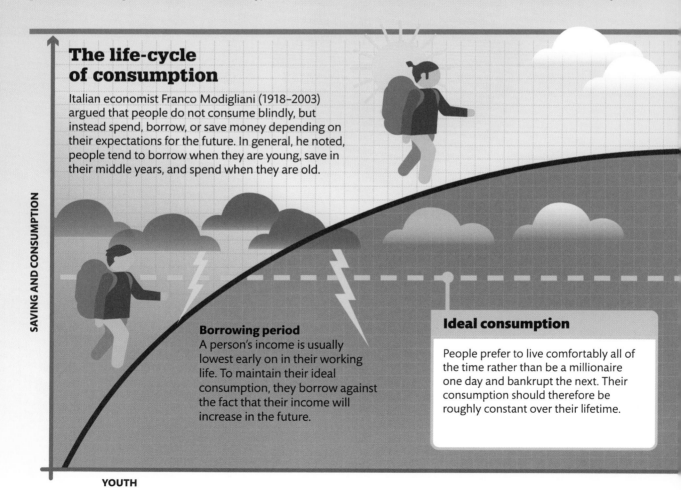

### The life-cycle of consumption

Italian economist Franco Modigliani (1918–2003) argued that people do not consume blindly, but instead spend, borrow, or save money depending on their expectations for the future. In general, he noted, people tend to borrow when they are young, save in their middle years, and spend when they are old.

SAVING AND CONSUMPTION

**Borrowing period**
A person's income is usually lowest early on in their working life. To maintain their ideal consumption, they borrow against the fact that their income will increase in the future.

**Ideal consumption**
People prefer to live comfortably all of the time rather than be a millionaire one day and bankrupt the next. Their consumption should therefore be roughly constant over their lifetime.

YOUTH

their current consumption. The situation is more complicated for savers. If the interest rate on savings increases, then there is a greater incentive for people to save, because the returns are greater. However, the more money they save, the more likely it is that they will decide to spend some of it.

## "Consumption smoothing leads to a hump-shaped pattern of wealth holding."

Franco Modigliani, Italian economist, Nobel Prize lecture (1985)

## INCOME CHANGES

A consequence of wanting to maintain a reasonably constant level of consumption is that temporary income changes have a limited impact on consumption, whereas permanent changes have a large and lasting effect. For example, if someone receives a $500 bonus at work and expects to live for another 50 years, then that bonus allows for only $10 of extra consumption per year. However, if they knew that they would receive an extra $500 each year until the end of their life, then their consumption would rise by the full $500 per year. In general, people tend to smooth their consumption around their expected long-term earnings.

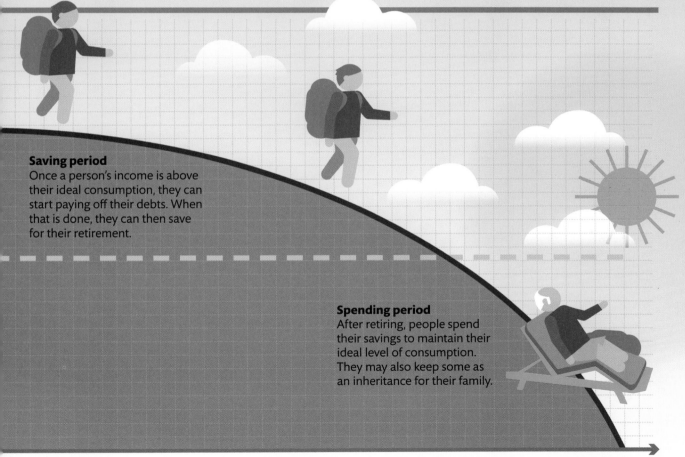

**Saving period**
Once a person's income is above their ideal consumption, they can start paying off their debts. When that is done, they can then save for their retirement.

**Spending period**
After retiring, people spend their savings to maintain their ideal level of consumption. They may also keep some as an inheritance for their family.

**MIDDLE AGE**

**OLD AGE**

# Business investment

**Firms invest money in order to grow in size or improve profitability. They may use the investment to train existing staff or hire new ones, purchase better equipment, develop new products, or enter new markets.**

## Types of investment

Firms invest in capital (staff or equipment) in order to reduce their production costs or improve their productive capacity (the number or quality of products or services they provide), with the aim of growing their sales or being more profitable. Investing in staff might involve training existing employees or hiring new ones to fulfill specific roles, while investing in equipment might mean an upgrade to current hardware or brand-new items.

Other routes firms use to grow sales and improve profitability is to invest in their products and services (either improving their existing ones or developing new ones) or expand into new markets, either by selling into new geographical regions or developing new areas of business.

## Funding investment

A firm can raise money for investment by using cash reserves, taking on debt, or issuing shares. But if a firm uses cash, it misses out on the return it would get from

## Investment options

To achieve growth or improve profitability, firms can invest in four main areas of business. These are staff, equipment, product development, and entering into new markets—all of which can be evaluated in terms of their net present value (NPV).

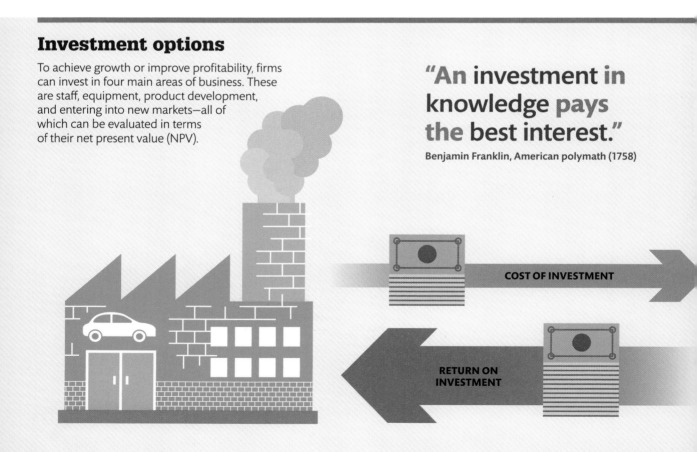

"An investment in knowledge pays the best interest."
Benjamin Franklin, American polymath (1758)

COST OF INVESTMENT

RETURN ON INVESTMENT

depositing the money in a bank or investing it in other opportunities, and if it takes on debt, it must make interest payments. The payment of dividends (see pp.194–195) to shareholders, however, is at the discretion of the firm. Other costs include the investment itself and, in the case of physical capital (such as equipment), its depreciation (loss of value) over time. For an investment to be worthwhile, it should generate a greater return than its cost.

## Weighing up investments

For each investment opportunity, a firm can calculate the total profit that investment will make over its lifetime by calculating its net present value (NPV) – see pp.76–77. The NPV of an investment equals its total estimated future income discounted to today's values, and minus its initial cost.

When estimating NPV, firms must take into account factors such as inflation, which reduces the value of money over time, and the cost of missed opportunity on other investments. Firms will generally try to fund any investments with a positive NPV, but where sources of funding are limited, they can use NPV to help them prioritize those investments that are likely to give the best returns.

### CASE STUDY

#### Apple iPhone

The first iPhone went on sale in the US in June 2007. A touchscreen mobile phone with few physical buttons, it was the first product of its kind. Its development took more than two years and cost around $150 million. But sales in 2007 alone were $630 million. Since then, many models have been released and more than 2.3 billion iPhones had been sold by the end of 2022.

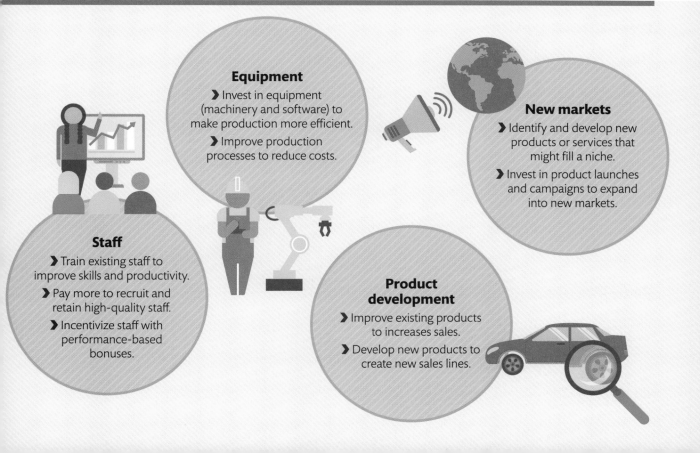

**Equipment**
> Invest in equipment (machinery and software) to make production more efficient.
> Improve production processes to reduce costs.

**New markets**
> Identify and develop new products or services that might fill a niche.
> Invest in product launches and campaigns to expand into new markets.

**Staff**
> Train existing staff to improve skills and productivity.
> Pay more to recruit and retain high-quality staff.
> Incentivize staff with performance-based bonuses.

**Product development**
> Improve existing products to increases sales.
> Develop new products to create new sales lines.

# Financial instruments

**Contracts between firms or individuals that state that one party owes money to the other are called "financial instruments." These contracts can be sold to third parties, so they have a market value in themselves.**

## Debt-based instruments

A good example of a financial instrument is a mortgage, which is a loan from a bank to a private individual who promises to pay back the loan with interest over a set period of time. However, instead of waiting years for the debtor to repay the loan, the bank can sell the mortgage to an investor, who, having paid the bank a fee, picks up the debtor's payments. The contract that the investor makes with the bank is a type of "bond" (more specifically, a "mortgage-backed security") that in turn can be sold to other investors. The bond market (see pp.204–205) includes all forms of instruments based on debt.

## Equity-based instruments

Other types of financial instruments are based on equity—or property ownership—instead of debt. Shares, for example, represent equal parts of a company's capital, which means that anyone who owns a share owns a portion of the company. Shares are also of limited liability, which means that an investor can only lose the money they put in—they are not liable for the company's other debts. Companies distribute profits to shareholders by paying them dividends (see p.195).

### Shares
These represent partial ownership of a company. They can be traded between investors in secondary markets (see pp.194–195).

## Types of financial instruments

Bonds and shares are the main types of financial instruments, but there are plenty of others on the market. These range from currencies and derivatives to property and commodities such as metals, oil, and coffee.

### Buyers

Investors who are confident that an asset's value is about to rise tend to buy large amounts of the asset, believing that they can sell it for a higher price at a later date.

## "BULL" AND "BEAR" MARKETS

In financial markets, the terms "bull" and "bear" are commonly used to refer to market conditions. A "bull market" is characterized by rising asset prices, high sales volumes, and economic optimism, which reflects a positive economy. Whereas, a "bear market" is associated with falling asset prices, stagnant sales volumes, and economic pessimism.

## KEY MARKETS/ASSETS

### Bonds
A bond is a promise to repay a lender a particular amount of money on a particular date, plus regular interest payments.

### Currencies
These are bought and sold for international trade, cross-border investing, and speculation (see pp.212–213).

### Derivatives
These are assets that derive their value from other assets. They typically involve the obligation or option to buy or sell something in the future.

### Other assets
Property and commodities such as oil and gas (as well as derivatives of these) are also tradable financial assets.

### Sellers
Investors who are confident that an asset's value is about to fall tend to sell as much of the asset as they can, believing that it will only drop in price.

### Borrowers
Some investors pay fees to borrow assets, which they then sell, believing that their price will drop—in which case, they then rebuy the assets at a cheaper price and return them to their owners.

# Financial markets

As the name suggests, financial markets are marketplaces where assets, such as stocks, bonds, and derivatives, can be traded. The New York Stock Exchange is arguably the best-known financial market in the world.

## Primary and secondary markets

The primary market is where new shares are created and issued (sold) to the public for the first time. Also known as "floating" a company on the stock market or "going public," this process can be carried out with an auction or with an initial public offering (IPO). In an IPO, an investment bank sets a price for an asset and investors can buy it from the bank at that price. Alternatively, firms can sell assets directly to investors.

Secondary markets are where investors can buy and sell assets that have already been issued, and include stock exchanges. Trades in secondary markets can be quote-driven or order-driven. For quote-driven trades, dealers advertise that they are willing to buy or sell a certain quantity of an asset at a given price. Traders pick the best price or try to negotiate with the dealer. In order-driven markets, investors enter orders saying they want to buy or sell a certain quantity of an asset, and these may be limit or market orders (see below).

## Limit and market orders

Limit buy orders are where an investor wants to buy a certain quantity of an asset but pay no more than a certain price. Similarly, limit sell orders are where an investor wants to sell a certain quantity of an asset for at least a certain price. Investors can also place market orders, where they buy or sell a certain quantity of an asset at the best available price.

**COMPANY "Y" SHARE**

$100

**INVESTOR A**

**Other orders**
At 5 p.m., Investor B places a limit order to sell 100 shares for at least $98 each.

**INVESTOR B**

**Placing an order**
At 2 p.m., Investor A places a limit order to buy 50 shares for up to $98 each—currently valued at $100 each.

# $25.6bn
## was the amount raised by oil company Saudi Aramco's IPO, the largest of all time

www.bloomberg.com, "Saudi Aramco Raises $25.6 Billion in World's Biggest IPO" (2019)

All assets have a buyer and a seller, and there are also brokers, who make trades on behalf of others in return for a fee.

## Asset returns

The return on an asset is the profit made when it was sold divided by its initial cost. An asset bought for $10 and sold for $12 has a 20 percent return ($2 profit divided by $10 initial cost). Leverage is where investors borrow to invest and it magnifies both gains and losses, which, in turn, adds risk.

## SHORT SELLING

"Shorting," or short selling, is a trading strategy where investors aim to profit from a decline in an asset's price. An investor borrows (for a fee) an asset they think will fall in value. They sell the borrowed asset before the price falls. They then buy the asset back in the future to return it to the broker they borrowed it from. If the price falls as the short seller anticipates, they make a profit.

BROKER — Borrows shares for a fee → Returns shares ← SHORT SELLER — Sells at current market price → Buys back shares at a later price ← MARKET

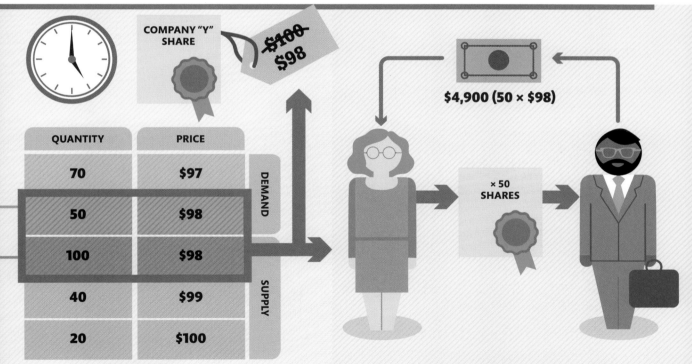

### Order matching
There is now someone willing to sell 50 shares at $98 a share to Investor A. Investor B's sell limit order for the remaining 50 shares at $98 stays on the order book, a real-time list of orders.

### Trade executed
Ownership of 50 of Investor B's shares is transferred to Investor A, and 50 x $98 is transferred to Investor B. The market price of Y's share reflects the latest trade and drops to $98.

COMPANY "Y" SHARE

~~$100~~ $98

$4,900 (50 × $98)

× 50 SHARES

| QUANTITY | PRICE |
|----------|-------|
| 70 | $97 |
| 50 | $98 |
| 100 | $98 |
| 40 | $99 |
| 20 | $100 |

DEMAND

SUPPLY

ORDER BOOK

# Risk

Investors cannot compare assets solely in terms of the returns that they expect to make. Because future prices of assets are unknown, investors must also compare their risk—the likelihood of financial loss.

### Measuring risk

Since most people are averse to risk, it is reasonable to assume that, if two assets have the same expected return, but one is less risky, then most people will choose the asset that has the lower risk attached to it. Riskier assets have what economists call a higher "risk premium," which is the difference between the asset's expected return and the return on a risk-free, or extremely low-risk, asset of the same value, such as a short-term government bond (see pp.204–205).

The return on an asset is its future price, minus its current price, divided by its current price.

Because the return depends on an unknown future price, it is uncertain, and investors therefore need a guide to measure the amount of risk attached to it. This guide is known as the "variance," which measures the range of possible returns on an asset weighted by the likelihood of the

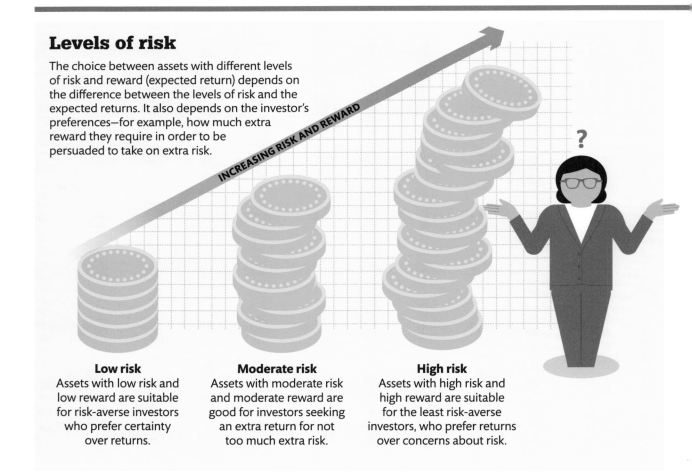

## Levels of risk

The choice between assets with different levels of risk and reward (expected return) depends on the difference between the levels of risk and the expected returns. It also depends on the investor's preferences—for example, how much extra reward they require in order to be persuaded to take on extra risk.

INCREASING RISK AND REWARD

**Low risk**
Assets with low risk and low reward are suitable for risk-averse investors who prefer certainty over returns.

**Moderate risk**
Assets with moderate risk and moderate reward are good for investors seeking an extra return for not too much extra risk.

**High risk**
Assets with high risk and high reward are suitable for the least risk-averse investors, who prefer returns over concerns about risk.

most extreme outcomes (very high or very low returns). The variance reflects both the "upside" and the "downside" risk of an investment. The upside risk is the chance that the asset's return will be higher than the investor expected—the downside risk is the opposite.

## Investor preferences

The most common measure of an asset's downside risk is known as its "conditional value at risk," or CVaR (see below). This gives investors an idea of the shortfall that they might expect on making a given investment or on holding onto an asset.

The most appropriate measure of risk will depend on the investor's preferences. If an investor is aiming to make a certain amount of money from an investment, for example, to buy a house, then they will be more sensitive to the downside risk. The upside risk of making more money than they need will be less important to them.

# 8.3%
## was the average risk premium for US stocks 1946–2022

Kenneth French, American professor of finance

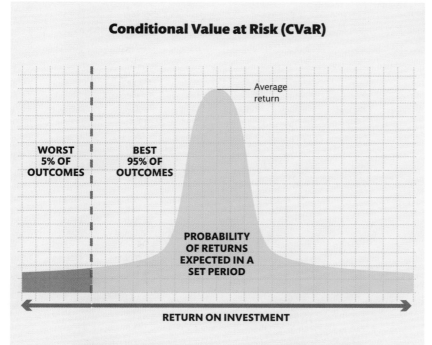

**Conditional Value at Risk (CVaR)**

Average return

WORST 5% OF OUTCOMES

BEST 95% OF OUTCOMES

PROBABILITY OF RETURNS EXPECTED IN A SET PERIOD

RETURN ON INVESTMENT

CVaR is a statistic that measures the potential losses within a firm or investment portfolio over a given period of time. Specifically, it quantifies the expected losses in the worst-case scenarios so that investors know how much they may lose if they invest in a particular asset. For example, a 5 percent CVaR is the expected return in the worst 5 percent of outcomes.

## RISK AND UNCERTAINTY

In economics, the terms "risk" and "uncertainty" have slightly different meanings—and risk is defined in a variety of ways.

> **Risk** An assessment of an asset when the outcome is unknown but the probability of each possible outcome is known.

> **Uncertainty** An assessment of an asset when both the outcome and the probability of each outcome are unknown.

> **Price risk** The risk that an asset's future price may not be what was expected.

> **Default risk** The risk that a borrower may not repay a debt.

> **Inflation risk** The risk that high inflation may erode the real value of an asset.

> **Exchange rate risk** The risk that the home currency value of a foreign asset may not be what was expected due to fluctuations in the currency market.

# Stock prices

The price of stocks rises and falls according to demand, which in turn is driven by risk and the preferences and expectations of investors. Ultimately, stock prices reflect expected future dividends.

## Supply and demand

As in any other market, stock prices are determined by supply and demand, but generally they are influenced by the latter instead of the former. This is because stock prices are mainly driven by changes in investor demand (see below). Supply only becomes a factor when firms issue new shares. However, this is rare, because newly issued shares dilute those of existing shareholders.

A firm might issue new shares if something happens that makes it want to invest more—such as a change in regulations or taxes or the emergence of a new product that it wants to invest in. Alternatively, the firm can raise money by going into debt.

## Investor preferences

Many things shift investor demand for a stock. If investors' expectations of a firms's future performance improve, then demand for the stock will increase (see pp.106–107). However, the risk of the stock relative to the investors' other assets is also important. If a stock becomes less risky compared to others—because its own risk falls or the others' rises—demand for the stock will increase. Investor preferences are equally important: if investors want to take less risk, then the demand for riskier stocks will fall.

## How stock prices work

Demand for stock comes from people wanting to buy shares when they are first issued by firms, or on the secondary market, where ownership of shares is transferred.

**DEMAND**

### Increase in demand
If demand for shares outstrips their supply, their price will rise until investors no longer want to buy them. Some investors may decide to sell them before their price falls.

**SUPPLY**

Likewise, if investors disapprove of particular firms—possibly because they cause pollution—then demand for their shares will fall.

## STOCKS OR SHARES?

The terms "stock" and "share" are used interchangeably to mean an asset that represents partial ownership of a public company. However, the term "stock" also means a collection of shares: investors buy shares of a company's stock.

## DIVIDENDS

Profits earned by a firm that are distributed to its shareholders are known as dividends. Payments are discretionary, but because the shareholders own the company, the firm has to distribute its profits to the shareholders at some point. The firm's total profits equal the value of all of the dividends it eventually pays. The price of the stock is the expected value of all current and future dividends. Expected future dividends are worth less (see pp.76–77) because future money is not as valuable to investors as current money.

Firm announces profit → Firm makes decision on dividend → Firm keeps some money for investment / Firm pays dividends

# $565 bn dividend payments
## were made by S&P 500 companies in 2022
www.investopedia.com

**DEMAND**

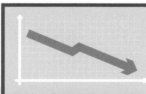

### Increase in supply
If a firm issues more shares but demand does not change, the share price falls until all of the shares are sold.

**SUPPLY**

# Efficient market hypothesis

**According to the efficient market hypothesis (EMH), stock prices reflect fully and fairly all available market information—and therefore no one has access to knowledge that would let them consistently "beat" the market.**

## An uncertain future

Imagine if it were possible to predict that a stock price would rise in three months' time. With this knowledge, investors would buy the stock, increasing its price as a result. Investors would keep buying the stock until its current price became so high that no one wanted to buy it anymore. The stock price would not then rise in three months' time, or it might rise only a little.

This paradoxical series of events shows how, according to the EMH, stock-price changes are hard to predict and future returns are unforecastable. At the heart of the hypothesis is the idea that all the information that is relevant to stock prices is freely available to all investors and, therefore, is accurately reflected in the price of stocks. In other words, the "efficient market" is a level playing field where no one can know what new information will be released and make a profit from it (unless they are engaging in the illegal practice known as "insider trading"); any profit made is therefore a lucky, one-off event.

## The EMH in practice

When new information arises, the theory states, stock prices adjust in almost real time as investors compete to trade as quickly as they can. A good example of this happened when the Challenger space shuttle exploded in 1986. Within 13 minutes, the share price of the project's four main contractors had fallen 4–6 percent. By the end of the day's trading, shares in one firm, Morton-Thiokol, were down 12 percent. It took another five months for an official report to name problems with a Morton-Thiokol component as a key factor in the explosion. This example illustrates the wisdom of the market itself, which "knows" better than the traders who are trying to outsmart it.

## ARGUMENTS AGAINST THE EFFICIENT MARKET HYPOTHESIS

> **Irrational investors** The EMH assumes that investors process information rationally and trade accordingly. Experts in behavioral finance (see pp.198–199) argue that the theory fails to account for the errors in human reasoning that can affect trading decisions. Also, not all investors look at stocks in the same way. Some might see growth potential in a stock, while others view it as overvalued.

> **Successful investors** Some people outperform the market. For example, US billionaire investor Warren Buffet beat the market for 39 out of 58 years up to 2023. If markets were truly "efficient," such huge success would be impossible.

## Can we ever predict returns?

A stock market can only react to events, not predict them. According to the EMH, a stock price reflects what is known now, with a rise or fall in value only following good or bad news. The exception to this "efficient" market is the role played in stock predictability by levels of risk (see pp.192–193). Changes in a stock's risk will affect the demand for the stock, which in turn will affect its price.

# 95% of active US equity funds failed to beat the market between 2002 and 2022

S&P Dow Jones Indices (2022)

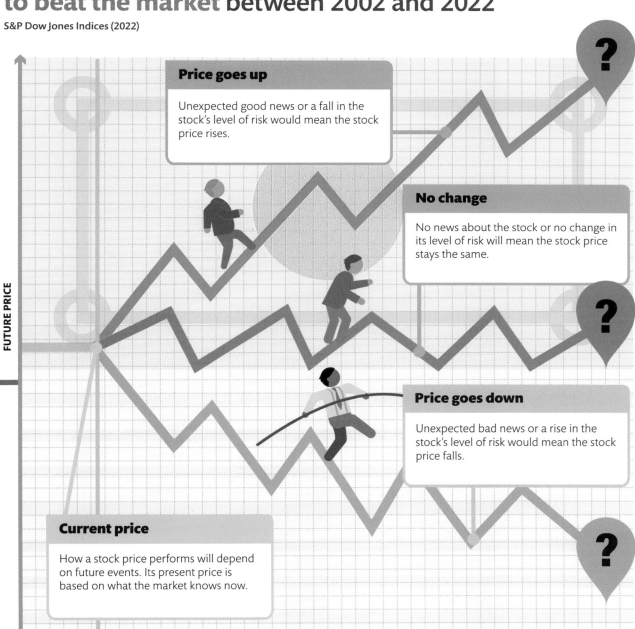

**Price goes up**

Unexpected good news or a fall in the stock's level of risk would mean the stock price rises.

**No change**

No news about the stock or no change in its level of risk will mean the stock price stays the same.

**Price goes down**

Unexpected bad news or a rise in the stock's level of risk would mean the stock price falls.

**Current price**

How a stock price performs will depend on future events. Its present price is based on what the market knows now.

FUTURE PRICE

PERFORMANCE TO DATE

TIME

# Behavioral finance

Occasionally, investors make decisions that go against the traditional logic of the market, so they seem irrational. The branch of economics that studies such decisions is known as "behavioral finance."

## Rational and irrational investors

Whether investors are trading on their own account or managing money for clients, they are all human, so they make unpredictable decisions—and these can cause stock prices to deviate from what their dividends state they should be (see pp.194–195).

However, rational investors can learn from such anomalies and trade against them accordingly. For example, due to what is known as the "availability bias," many investors only buy stock from companies they are familiar with. Such companies, though, may only be familiar because they have a high public profile,

## Behavioral biases

Psychologists have documented a variety of irrational behaviors, or "behavioral biases," that investors are prone to. These cause investors to trade in ways that are not in their best interests and cause prices to depart from what they should be under the efficient markets hypothesis (see pp.196–197). By understanding these biases, rational investors can profit from irrational ones.

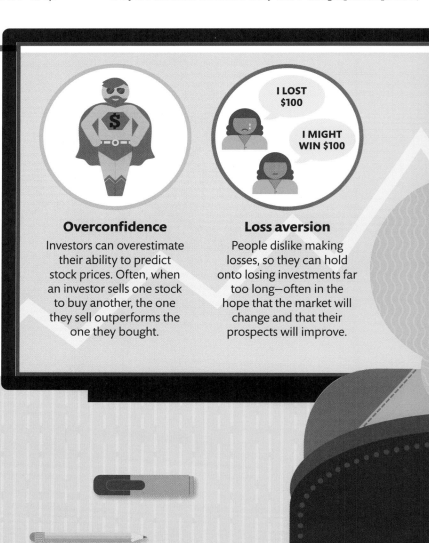

### Overconfidence
Investors can overestimate their ability to predict stock prices. Often, when an investor sells one stock to buy another, the one they sell outperforms the one they bought.

### Loss aversion
People dislike making losses, so they can hold onto losing investments far too long—often in the hope that the market will change and that their prospects will improve.

## UNPREDICTABILITY

Behavioral psychologists claim that the market is more like a person than a machine—in other words, is capable of extreme swings of behavior that make it far less predictable than economists have traditionally believed. However, although this view offers valuable insights into why the market has been volatile in the past, it has yet to provide investors with strategies for dealing with such "mood swings" in the future.

which means that many people buy their stocks, which in turn often become overpriced. Knowing these facts, a rational investor can short sell such stocks if they are selling well and make a profit when their price begins to fall (see pp.190–191)—after which any further short selling becomes unprofitable. In such circumstances, both the share price and the behavior of irrational investors are corrected by rational investors.

There are many instances in which stock prices are damaged because rational investors are unable to correct them. This can be due to the fact that investors are limited in what they can trade—maybe because they cannot raise sufficient funds to buy enough of an undervalued stock to increase its price. Alternatively, they may be limited in how much they can short—if, for example, the fees for short selling are too high, or not enough stockholders are willing to lend their stock. In such circumstances, overvalued stock prices are prevented from falling and remain artificially high. Prices may also fail to correct because there is too much irrational trading, in which case rational investors make losses.

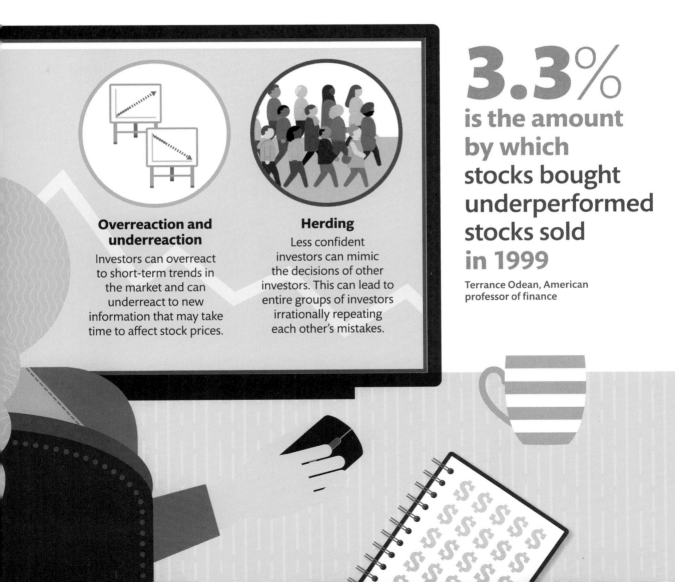

### Overreaction and underreaction
Investors can overreact to short-term trends in the market and can underreact to new information that may take time to affect stock prices.

### Herding
Less confident investors can mimic the decisions of other investors. This can lead to entire groups of investors irrationally repeating each other's mistakes.

## 3.3%
is the amount by which stocks bought underperformed stocks sold in 1999

Terrance Odean, American professor of finance

# Economic bubbles

When the prices of goods rapidly rise far above their true value, the result is an economic bubble. In finance, bubbles occur when investors buy overpriced assets and sell them at even higher prices.

## Rational bubbles

Asset prices are related to their "fair and expected prices," or "fundamentals." Stock prices, for example, reflect their expected future dividends (see pp.194–195). However, assets sometimes become dramatically overpriced, thanks to irrational speculation (see pp.98–99) by investors who believe—without real evidence—that the market for a particular asset is trending in an unusually favorable direction. In such circumstances, investing in the asset is an act of faith—and yet it is rational for an investor to buy it if they believe that they can sell it at an even higher price in the future. They risk the bubble bursting—and the price correcting—before they can sell the asset, but if the probability of that happening is low, it is rational for them to "ride the bubble." Another way of making money from a bubble is by betting against it, or short selling (see pp.190–191). However, short selling is risky—very often, what seems to be a bubble is in fact the asset increasing in real value.

## The financial instability hypothesis

American economist Hyman Minsky (1919–1996) believed that financial bubbles occur because stability breeds instability. In economically stable times, he argued, bad investments are

## The life cycle of bubbles

Economic bubbles come and go in cycles that affect all kinds of assets, including shares, bonds, and commodities (see pp.188–189). They begin with investors learning of a new investment opportunity, and often end after a single, minor-seeming event. Hyman Minsky identified five key stages in these cycles.

### Fundamental value

The fundamental value of an asset is its fair price—in other words, the price it would trade at under normal market conditions.

### Displacement

An unexpected change (displacement) in the market, such as a drop in interest rates, increases the value of an asset.

### Boom

The price of the asset rises rapidly. This receives a lot of media attention, prompting investors to buy the asset in large quantities.

relatively rare, so risk-taking becomes more and more attractive. Investors then become complacent and start taking excessive risks—which causes bubbles that eventually burst. The chaos of the resulting crash deters investors from taking risks for a while, but the memory of what happened eventually fades and the cycle starts again. Minsky noted that the most economically stable periods are always followed by the worst crashes because the greater the stability, the more excessive the risk-taking.

## CASE STUDY

### *Nonfungible tokens*

In 2014, assets known as a "nonfungible tokens" (NFTs) first appeared on the market. These gave investors ownership of all kinds of irreplaceable (nonfungible) items, such as works of art. However, the global market for specifically art-related NFTs almost halved in value from $2.9 billion in 2021 to $1.5 billion in 2022. It had risen from only $70 million in 2020, leading many to argue it had been a bubble. The broader NFT market suffered far less of a decline in value in 2022.

**Euphoria**
Investors believe that there will always be people willing to buy the asset, even as its price rises to precariously high levels.

**Profit-taking**
Cautious investors, sensing that the bubble will burst, start selling the asset and banking their profits.

**Panic**
The bubble bursts as more and more investors sell the asset, causing its price to fall to its original, fundamental level.

"The last century proves that ... irrationality of an extreme kind periodically erupts."
Warren Buffett, American investor (2021)

# Optimal portfolios

The ideal, or "optimal portfolio," investment will deliver the most appropriate balance of risk and reward. Investors can use the capital asset pricing model (CAPM) to assess the best investment to make.

## Risk and reward

Most investments carry risk, and their returns tend to reflect this: risk-takers can be rewarded with higher returns, whereas low-risk assets return only small rewards. Investors generally aim to balance risk and reward in order to get either the highest possible return for their acceptable level of risk or the lowest possible risk for their desired expected return.

The capital asset pricing model (CAPM) predicts expected returns and is based on three metrics: the "safe rate," the "market risk," and the "company's risk." The safe rate (also known as the "risk-free" rate) is the safest way to invest, such as using a savings account. The market risk is based on the overall risk of the stock market or sector. The company's risk is based on the risk of the specific company or asset. Some are riskier than others because they are smaller or are in a more volatile industry.

## The efficient frontier

In 1952, the American economist Harry Markowitz (1927–2023) introduced the concept of the "efficient frontier." It is a way to model an ideal set of portfolios that have the optimum ratio of risk and reward: they provide the highest expected returns for a given risk or the lowest risk for a given return.

"A good portfolio is more than a long list of good stocks and bonds. It is a balanced whole ..."

Harry Markowitz, *Portfolio Selection* (1959)

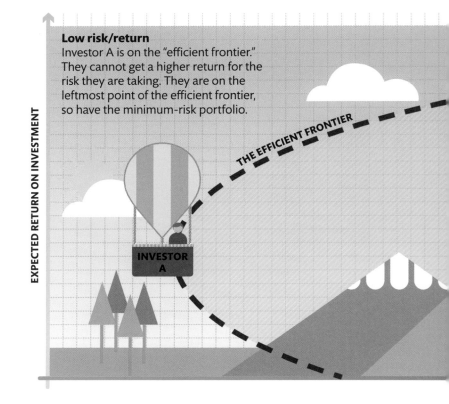

**Low risk/return**
Investor A is on the "efficient frontier." They cannot get a higher return for the risk they are taking. They are on the leftmost point of the efficient frontier, so have the minimum-risk portfolio.

THE EFFICIENT FRONTIER

EXPECTED RETURN ON INVESTMENT

INVESTOR A

## Diversifying risk

A common way to reduce the risk of investments is to invest in a "portfolio" of companies or assets, usually spread across industries and with a range of risk profiles.

Investments that tend to follow the direction of the stock market are said to have a "positive correlation" with it. They provide little protection when the market does poorly, so they have a higher risk premium. An asset that performs well when everything else does badly offers insurance against market downturns, so it has a lower risk premium.

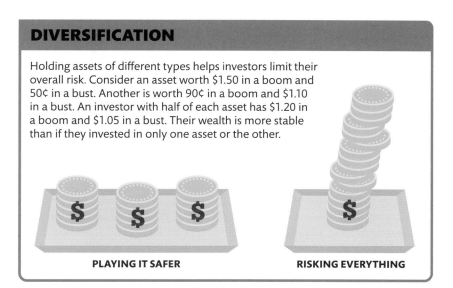

## DIVERSIFICATION

Holding assets of different types helps investors limit their overall risk. Consider an asset worth $1.50 in a boom and 50¢ in a bust. Another is worth 90¢ in a boom and $1.10 in a bust. An investor with half of each asset has $1.20 in a boom and $1.05 in a bust. Their wealth is more stable than if they invested in only one asset or the other.

**PLAYING IT SAFER**

**RISKING EVERYTHING**

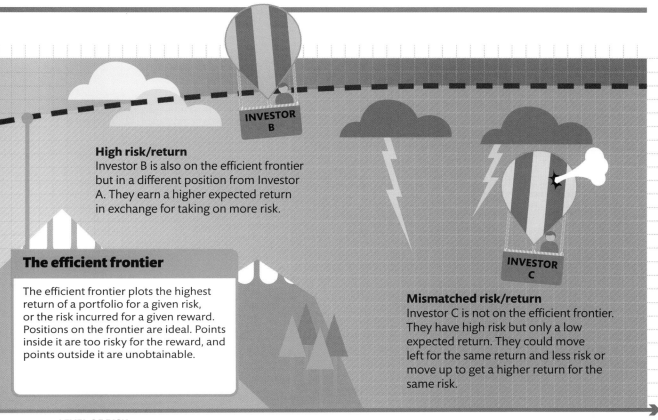

### High risk/return
Investor B is also on the efficient frontier but in a different position from Investor A. They earn a higher expected return in exchange for taking on more risk.

### The efficient frontier

The efficient frontier plots the highest return of a portfolio for a given risk, or the risk incurred for a given reward. Positions on the frontier are ideal. Points inside it are too risky for the reward, and points outside it are unobtainable.

### Mismatched risk/return
Investor C is not on the efficient frontier. They have high risk but only a low expected return. They could move left for the same return and less risk or move up to get a higher return for the same risk.

**LEVEL OF RISK**

# Bond markets

A bond is a contract that a government or firm can make with an investor to raise money. It is effectively a loan that the investor makes in return for a fixed rate of interest.

### Face and market value

When an investor buys a bond, they receive a certificate that guarantees they will be repaid the face value of the bond (the amount it is worth) at a certain date in the future (the maturity date). The bond price is typically less than the face value because future money is less valuable than present money. The bond certificate may also guarantee that the issuer will pay them regular, fixed "coupon" payments in the meantime. The difference between the bond price and the face value, plus any coupon payments, make up the investor's profits—effectively the interest they are paid. The bond yield converts the total profit the investor makes into an annualized interest rate. Bond holders do not have to wait for their maturity dates to arrive. They can trade bonds because bonds have a market value as well as a price and face value. The market value reflects fluctuations in interest rates. Higher interest rates make money in the future less valuable than money today, causing bond prices to fall and yields to rise.

### Risk

Another factor that affects the price of bonds is risk. If a bond takes 10 years to mature, there

## How a bond works

The price of the bond is paid in full by the investor to the firm or government issuing the bond, which can then spend the money. The investor is then repaid through coupon payments and the face-value payment within a fixed period. The coupon payments are essentially interest payments on the loan.

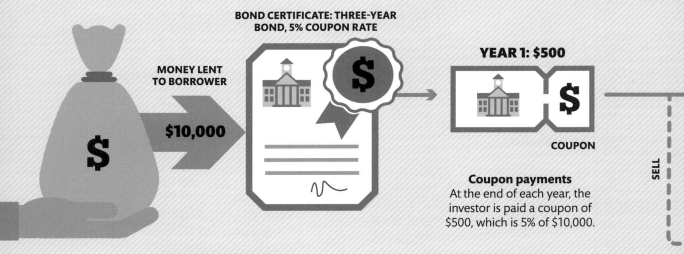

**MONEY LENT TO BORROWER**

**$10,000**

**BOND CERTIFICATE: THREE-YEAR BOND, 5% COUPON RATE**

**YEAR 1: $500**

**COUPON**

**Coupon payments**
At the end of each year, the investor is paid a coupon of $500, which is 5% of $10,000.

SELL

**Investing in bonds**
The investor buys the issuer's promise to repay $10,000 in three years' time, plus the coupons. The issuer is then legally bound to honor the promise.

is a risk that the issuer may go bankrupt before the maturity date. Government bonds are prized precisely because the state is generally a more stable institution and unlikely to renege on its obligations. Few investors have an appetite for risk, so high-risk bonds are the cheapest bonds of all.

## Inflation

Inflation also plays a role in how bonds are priced. High inflation erodes the real value of future payments, but if inflation looks likely to drop, then long-term loans become attractive to investors.

### YIELD CURVE INVERSION

A "yield curve inversion" occurs when government bonds with longer maturity times have lower yields than bonds with shorter ones. This is usually a bad sign because it suggests that investors are expecting interest rates to be cut, which is a measure that central banks take when a recession is imminent (see pp.94–95).

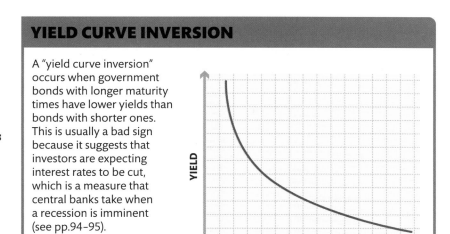

YIELD

MATURITY

## In 2022, the size of the worldwide bond market was

# $**133**trillion

World Economic Forum, "Ranked: The largest bond markets in the world" (2023)

**YEAR 2: $500**

COUPON

**YEAR 3: $500**

COUPON

**Option to sell**
If they want to get their money back early, the investor can sell the bond on the secondary market before maturity.

SOLD

**BOND'S FACE VALUE PAID TO INVESTOR**

$10,000

**Maturity date**
Once the bond matures at the end of the three years, the investor is paid the $10,000 face value plus the final $500 coupon.

# Derivatives

**Derivatives are financial contracts that fix a price in the present for a deal that will take place at a specified time in the future. The main types of derivatives are "forward" and "options."**

## Forward

A typical derivative is a "forward" contract, which is an agreement to buy or sell a commodity or asset for an agreed-on price at an agreed-on date in the future. This type of agreement can benefit producers if the market price of the commodity they are selling goes down over the specified period because they have locked their customers into a price ahead of time. Derivatives can therefore be used to reduce risk and insure against the future. But they can work the other way around, too, resulting in a loss for the producer and a gain for the customer if the market price of the commodity increases over the specified period of time.

In this way, derivatives can be used to gamble on the future, with speculators "buying forward" if they think something will rise in value and so make them a profit when they come to sell it. Forward contracts tend to be privately agreed on and, since they are not traded on exchanges, are called "over the counter" (OTC) deals.

## Options

Although similar to forward contracts, options are different in that the trade does not have to take place. The contract gives one party the option to buy or sell a certain amount of an asset or commodity in the future, but it does not force them to do so.

## Example of a forward deal

An orange juice producer enters into a forward contract with a farmer to reduce price uncertainty. By knowing in advance how much it will pay for oranges, the orange juice producer can have more certainty when setting its own prices.

**SUPPLY 5 TONS OF ORANGES AT $1,000/ TON**

### Farmer makes a deal with a juice-maker

The farmer agrees to sell the orange juice producer a set amount of oranges (5 tons) for a set price ($1,000 per ton) at a specified date (one year from now), making this a forward contract.

## NEED TO KNOW

❯ **Call option** The option to buy something for a specific price in the future.

❯ **Put option** The option to sell something for a specific price in the future.

❯ **European option** The option to buy or sell can only be exercised on the date specified in the contract.

❯ **American option** The option to buy or sell can be exercised at any time on or before the date specified in the contract.

## TYPES OF FORWARDS

❯ **Futures** Standardized forward contracts that are designed to be traded on exchanges; the seller can pay a fee to break the contract so delivery does not take place.

❯ **Repos** Short for "repurchase agreements"; a type of forward contract in which someone agrees to sell something, then buy it back again at a higher price on a specific date. It is a form of short-term borrowing.

❯ **Swaps** Another type of forward contract, swaps involve the exchange of one financial asset for another at a given point in time—for example, an interest-rate swap that involves the exchange of a fixed interest rate for a variable rate, or vice versa.

# $20.7 trillion
## of global OTC derivatives were held in December 2022

Bank for International Settlements (2023)

$5,000

5 TONS OF ORANGES

**One year later**
The trade takes place. The agreement is binding:
the farmer must sell 5 tons of oranges for
$1,000 per ton and the orange juice
producer must buy them at that price.

# Capital structure

A firm's capital structure is the proportion of debt (borrowed money) and equity (cash and company shares) that it uses to finance its activities. The right mix balances a number of different business needs.

## Debt and equity

Firms have two main sources of finance: debt and equity. Debt financing involves the firm borrowing (for example, from a bank), while equity financing involves the firm using its own cash. Capital structure is the mixture of debt and equity a firm uses for finance.

The Modigliani-Miller theory (see below) states that the overall value of the firm remains the same no matter what the ratio is between debt and equity.

However, this is an "idealized" model that links a firm's value and its capital structure, while the relationship between debt, equity, capital structure, and value is more complicated in the real world (see boxes opposite).

Finding a firm's optimal capital structure, or debt-to-equity ratio, therefore involves being able to find a balance between a number of different factors and various trade-offs.

## Modigliani-Miller theory

Based on a theoretical "ideal world" scenario with no special rules or taxes, this theory is an idealized benchmark for understanding the relationship between a firm's value and its capital structure. It states that the total value of the firm (represented by the pie here) remains the same whatever the ratio of debt to equity (the size of the two slices).

In the real world, however, external factors such as taxes can have a positive or negative effect on the use of debt versus equity, meaning that the ratio of the two will in turn affect the total value of the firm.

### Debt

Debt is money borrowed by a firm or individual, often with the obligation to repay the borrowed amount with interest over a set period.

In 2022, US firms outside the financial sector **had an average debt-to-equity ratio of more than**

# 84%

International Monetary Fund (2022)

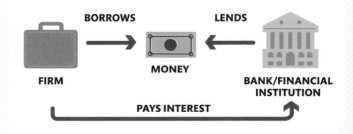

BORROWS     LENDS

MONEY

FIRM     BANK/FINANCIAL INSTITUTION

PAYS INTEREST

## PROS AND CONS OF DEBT

### Pros

> Any firm, whatever its size, can issue debt to "grow" its finances.

> Interest payments may be tax-deductible.

### Cons

> Interest payments could go up.

> Payments have to be made even in hard times.

> Greater risk of bankruptcy.

> Too much can affect the perceived value of the firm and its share price.

## PROS AND CONS OF EQUITY

### Pros

> No obligation to make dividend payments.

> Income is taxed less than debt income.

> Not likely to contribute toward bankruptcy.

### Cons

> Can dilute share value (by creating more overall shares).

> Can suggest managers do not expect the firm to perform well (they are not confident it would have been able to make debt repayments).

### Equity

Equity is made up of the value of a firm's shares and any cash it holds. Equity holders are paid out with dividends (see p.195), which are completely at the firm's discretion.

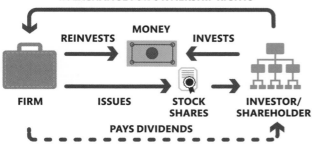

**IN EXCHANGE FOR OWNERSHIP RIGHTS**

REINVESTS    MONEY    INVESTS

FIRM    ISSUES    STOCK SHARES    INVESTOR/ SHAREHOLDER

PAYS DIVIDENDS

### Market value

According to the Modigliani-Miller theory, a firm's market value is the sum of its debt and its equity. The amount of debt can affect the size of the equity slice of the pie and the total value of the firm. However, the theory does not take into account real-world factors that affect a firm's market value, such as its financial performance, market conditions, and the pros and cons of debt and equity.

# Private equity and venture capital

**Privately owned firms and start-ups do not have the luxury of being able to finance themselves by selling public stock, but instead rely on venture capital and specialist investors.**

## Specialist investors

A private equity contract is one in which a specialist investment company buys a large share of a private company with a view to managing that company. The takeover is often largely financed by debt. The investment company sells shares in funds of its holdings of private companies to individual investors, who are also charged a fee. The minimum investment is usually high, and investors are unable to access their money for five or even 10 years. Although risky and initially very expensive, such investments can yield extremely good returns.

## Private equity

As well as funding private companies, private equity investors buy publicly listed companies. To buy a public company, an investor buys all of its shares, usually paying a premium over the current share price.

### Buying the firm
An investor who buys a firm takes the firm private—that is, stops the trade of its shares on the stock exchange.

### Managing the firm
The investor takes an active role in managing the firm, with the aim of making it more profitable.

### Selling the firm
Once the firm has been made more profitable—and its value has increased—the investor sells it for a profit.

## Venture capitalists

Many new firms, or start-ups, receive financing from specialist financiers known as venture capitalists. These start-ups tend to be in industries in which there is uncertainty about how big the market for their products will be or about the technology underlying their products. It is this uncertainty that deters traditional investors from providing start-ups with finance. Venture capital investing is therefore highly risky, but it can also bring high returns, which enables investors to bear a few losses. To reduce their risk, venture capitalists provide firms with valuable business advice and fund them in rounds so that they can monitor their progress in stages.

> "VC [venture capital] plays a critical role in taking start-ups to stardom."
>
> Ufuk Akcigit, Emin Dinlersoz, Jeremy Greenwood, and Veronica Penciakova, "Synergizing ventures," *Journal of Economic Dynamics and Control* (2022)

## Venture capital

Venture capitalists provide start-up firms with finance and advice. They may occasionally join a board of directors, but they rarely take full control. They may even finance firms jointly, so that they can pool their expertise.

FIRM INCREASES IN VALUE FROM $12.50 TO $125

40% SHARE OF $12.50—FIRM'S VALUE—BOUGHT FOR $5

$50 (40% OF $125)

40% SHARE

### Investing

A venture capitalist buys shares in a firm at an early stage of its development, when its prospects are uncertain.

### Advising

The investor provides the firm with money, advice, and oversight, helping it grow without managing it directly.

### Selling

Once the firm has grown and its prospects are secure, the investor sells their shares, expecting to make a profit.

# Currency exchanges

When one country buys goods or services from another, it usually pays using the currency of that country—which means it must first exchange an amount of its currency for theirs.

## Exchange rates

Modern international trade is only possible because currencies can be exchanged. However, currencies fluctuate in value. How much one is worth compared to another at a given time is called its exchange rate, which is usually quoted as how many units of a foreign currency the home currency can buy. Exchange rates are affected by how well or badly a country's economy is doing compared to another. Aggregate demand (AD) is the overall demand for goods and services in an economy, while aggregate supply (AS) is the overall supply of goods and services (see pp.102–103). If home AD increases relative to foreign AD while home and foreign AS stay the same, the home exchange rate appreciates (increases). It also appreciates if home AS decreases compared to foreign AS.

## What affects exchange rates?

Because exchange rates fluctuate, investors buy currencies specifically to exchange them with other currencies when exchange rates become more favorable. How much demand there is for a currency is determined by expectations about its future performance based on many factors. Positive factors will make the currency appreciate; negative factors will cause it to depreciate.

**APPRECIATION**

**APPRECIATION OR DEPRECIATION**

### Free-trade agreements

A new free-trade agreement creates expectations of a long-term currency appreciation, so the currency will appreciate.

### Interest rates

Interest rate changes (see p.115) affect the rates for government bonds. If rates rise, the currency appreciates; if rates fall, it depreciates.

### Speculation

If investors expect a currency to appreciate, they buy it to sell later, which causes an appreciation. The reverse causes a depreciation.

## Uncovered interest parity

The key relationship for determining exchange rates is uncovered interest parity (UIP), which is based on the interest rates for government bonds (see pp.204–205). The expected returns on foreign bonds are the foreign interest rate plus the expected depreciation of the home currency, because the returns on the foreign bond must be changed back into the home currency. The investor will buy either domestic or foreign bonds depending on which has the highest expected return. Because foreign bonds must be bought in the foreign currency, this purchase increases demand for the foreign currency, so the home currency depreciates (decreases) against it.

If anything increases the risk (see pp.192–193) of home bonds relative to foreign ones, investors will prefer foreign bonds; therefore, the home currency will depreciate.

## Currency pairings

Exchange rates can be defined between any two currencies. The US dollar is the currency most often used for comparison. Other major currencies also include the Euro and the Chinese yuan.

### ✓ NEED TO KNOW

> **Exchange rate** How much one currency can buy of another currency. For example, if £1 buys $1.20 (and $1 costs £0.83), then the pound-to-dollar exchange rate is 1.20.

> **Appreciation** When one currency increases in value compared to another. For example, if the pound-to-dollar exchange rate increases from 1.20 to 1.22, the pound has appreciated—£1 now buys $1.22 (and $1 costs £0.80).

> **Depreciation** When one currency decreases in value compared to another, as the dollar does in the example above.

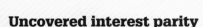

DEPRECIATION

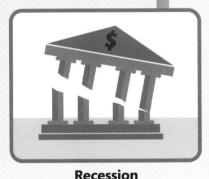

### Recession

Recession (see pp.94–95) causes bond interest rates to fall. Home bonds are less attractive than foreign bonds, so the currency depreciates.

### Government debt

Excessive debt increases the risk of the government defaulting on its loans (see pp.112–113). Bonds become riskier, and the currency depreciates.

### Political instability

Political instability increases the risk of a government defaulting on its debt. Its bonds become riskier, and the currency depreciates.

# Cryptocurrency

**A cryptocurrency is a form of virtual money that is exchanged and transferred digitally instead of through a bank. It relies on technological solutions to ensure trustworthy transactions.**

## A chain of digital money

Money is usually linked to a commodity (such as gold or silver) or issued and guaranteed by a bank, while a cryptocurrency is invisible and beyond the control of any financial body. A cryptocurrency takes the form of digital tokens, which exist on a digital network, where they can be bought and sold—using "real" money—or exchanged. Tokens can be used to buy goods and services, but they are mostly traded by investors through cryptocurrency exchanges.

Without the backing of a commodity or official assurance, cryptocurrency is open to fraud. Unlike cash or a precious metal, digital tokens can be easily copied for reuse, known as "double spending." To instill trust in the system, there has to be a record of token creation and transfer to confirm that tokens are unique. This is done by creating a public record of transactions—stored as blocks of data to form a "blockchain"—which users of the currency maintain instead of a central authority. Once added to the blockchain, data cannot be altered.

## Building the blockchain

All cryptocurrency transactions—including those of the largest currency, Bitcoin—are recorded in a blockchain, a public document distributed among and maintained by thousands of users. To make sure new entries are trustworthy, each block of transactions is verified through the solution to a mathematical puzzle, then added to the chain.

### Transaction requested

An individual requests a Bitcoin transaction. For example, one user wants to transfer tokens to another to pay for goods or services.

### Block created

Bitcoin miners compare the request with their blockchain copy to check for double spending. They stack legitimate transactions into blocks.

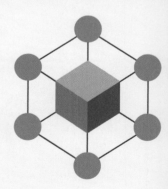

### Block sent out

Once a new block is complete, miners broadcast it to the network together with the solution to a mathematical puzzle.

## Verifying the chain

The blockchain is not infallible—a user could submit a false update to gain fake "new" tokens. To avoid this, the cryptocurrency network sets a digitally generated mathematical puzzle based on the previous block in the chain. Individuals or pools of individuals known as "miners" compete to solve the puzzle using complex computer hardware and software. Once "miners" have verified a transaction, they broadcast this and the puzzle solution to the cryptocurrency network and are rewarded with digital tokens.

In theory, mining makes it impossible to create a false blockchain. It would have to be longer than the existing blockchain to be credible, costing too much in computing power, time, and money to be worthwhile.

### CONTROVERSIES

> **Economic impact** The value of a cryptocurrency is much more volatile than that of a regular currency, such as the Euro or US dollar. This makes it a highly risky investment, with the potential for huge financial losses.

> **Illegal transactions** As there is no banking system behind a cryptocurrency, it is impossible for financial regulators to block potentially illegal transactions.

> **Environmental impact** Cryptocurrency mining requires a huge amount of computing power and energy. This creates significant carbon dioxide emissions and generates high levels of computer hardware waste.

# 2140 is the year when, it is estimated, the final "mined" Bitcoin will be added to the blockchain

www.investopedia.com, 2023

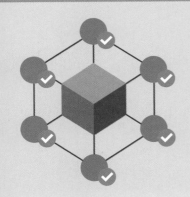

### Block validated
Other miners check that the answer to the puzzle is correct. The solution depends on the solutions to all previous blockchain puzzles.

### Block added to blockchain
Once the miners confirm the solution is correct, they add the block to their copy of the blockchain.

### Record created
Details of the original transaction, including amount, time, and date, are now publicly available as a digital record.

# Index

# N

# O

# P